MAD ABOUT MEN

MAD ABOUT MEN

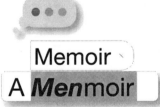

Memoir

A *Men*moir

MADELYN MORGAN

DISCLAIMER

New genre alert! This is a work of creative-memoir-nonfiction-biography-humor type thingy. The events and characters portrayed here are to the best of Madelyn's (distorted) memory, and she cannot claim pure accuracy. While all the stories in the book are mostly true, names and identifying details have been changed to protect the privacy of the assholes...I mean...people involved. Some stories and dialogue have been fictionalized to varying degrees for various purposes, sometimes at the expense of the joke. Trust me, it's better this way for everyone's sake.

Book Design by Ashley Prine, Tandem Books

Library of Congress Catalog-in-Publication Data has been applied for.
ISBN-10: 0-9982977-0-4
ISBN-13: 978-0-9982977-0-5

www.madaboutmen.com

SECOND EDITION

FIRST EDITION DECEMBER 2016

Dedicated to "Tyrone."
Sigh...or whomever.

• • •

Seriously, though.
For Imogen,
the true love of my life.

CONTENTS

CHAPTER 1
BANG!

My editor said I needed to start this book with a bang. So here goes…

One day, I had phenomenal sex with a particularly gorgeous personal trainer from my gym. He had the most stunningly perfect body, as those trainers tend to have. Caramel skin, abs like you read about in *Six Pack* magazine, thick, gorgeous, kissable lips, tricep cuts— one of my favorite parts of a fit man's body—and the perfect-sized dick with a sweet little tattoo of unknown design in that sexy area just below his perfectly protruding hip bone.

We had been flirting hard for several months, until one Saturday afternoon at the gym we hugged each other "hello" so tightly that it was obvious something else was brewing.

After we had a spontaneous lunch together that same day, we went for a long walk along the Manhattan waterfront, held hands, and made out like high-schoolers. When he walked me back to my apartment there was very little discussion about what would be happening next.

I had been wanting to be properly laid for a long time. It's not that I wasn't having sex regularly with my then-boyfriend; it was just bad sex. One-way sex. I was in a rut and needed my world rocked, which it was on that day, multiple times.

I'm not sure if this is what my editor meant by start the book with a bang.

• • •

So, now let me back up and introduce myself. Wait. First, did you read *Eat, Pray, Love*? I know, I know, stop gagging. You may roll your eyes at that reference, or you can just admit that it was an excellent read and her journey was amazing and the book was brilliant, but it was just that disappointing movie that's making you react negatively. Anyway, early in the book, Elizabeth Gilbert didn't recount the details of her marriage's end. She gave you just enough of the story so you could follow along on her journey. So, I think a nice bullet-point summary will bring you up to speed here.

- I work in the music business.
- I married a guy I met through work.
- I had a miscarriage, then had a genius-perfect-child, then another miscarriage. One for three—that was enough of that pregnancy madness.
- Four years after genius-perfect-daughter's arrival, I had started a new job in which I was expected to deliver big results. This involves generally having your shit together. Upon my beginning said job, within a six-month period of time:
  - My husband left me.

- My mother died.
- My sister died.

That kind of shit seriously fucks with you. One or maybe two of those things happening in a year is bad enough. But I felt like the dump truck of hell had just backed up making that annoying beeping noise, positioned itself right over me, reared up, and unloaded a full bed of steaming, hellish contents on my head, stopped beeping, and then drove off.

To elaborate on the bullets a bit: I had been chugging along in my relatively stable life up to that point. I had already enjoyed a long and successful career in the music business, doing exactly what I'd set out to do as a teenager. I started out at a radio station, then followed my dream to work at a record label. Over the years, I've worked for twelve different labels, handling marketing and promotion for musical artists of all genres, all sizes, famous and developing, in all styles of rock, pop, R&B, alternative, and the rest of whatever is considered contemporary at the moment. It's been a varied, multi-genre successful career. I'm hot shit in my job.

Mid-career, I met my best friend in the whole world. He played guitar in one of the bands that I was responsible for marketing. Before we met, I saw him in a photograph. I immediately zeroed in on him and said to myself, "THAT is someone interesting that I'm going to be friends with." I was inexplicably drawn to him in that photo. And when we first met, the magic was indeed there in person. When you hear about that kind of connection, it's usually in a chick flick or some kind of bullshit *Cinderella* situation. Deep down, you don't really believe that meant-to-be crap happens in real life. In this case, the guy was married when we met, thus proving my point. However, fate slapped me upside the head in an attempt to prove me wrong.

There was no avoiding it. He knew it. I knew it. Everyone knew it. We were soul mates. After about a year of us pretending to be "really great friends," he left his wife and moved from the Midwest to New York City, directly into my apartment. I had never understood love and happiness like this before. So *this* was what all the fuss was about. After the three aforementioned attempts at building a family, we decided that one perfect child plus the two of us in our perfect marriage equaled maximum happiness. He opted to stay home with our daughter so that he could freely work on his music, while I held down a few different record company jobs through the years and brought home the proverbial bacon. We had one of those rare relationships; we made each other laugh constantly and had all the same interests and were deeply connected sexually and mentally and were just completely in love. Friends thought we spoke our own language and we were definitely one of those annoying couples who constantly quip inside jokes to each other. The three of us were a super-tight family unit of love and supreme happiness.

I never really, truly understood exactly why he left. How was it even possible? To his credit, he agreed that we should meet with a therapist together. But, to his discredit, his purpose in those meetings was to explain to me why he

4

was leaving rather than identify the issues between us and work to fix them. He was fully ready to split, end of story.

A marriage like that, you'd think would be worth attempting to save, but he wasn't interested in that. And even after the therapy sessions, I still didn't understand why. Was it me? Was I too consumed with work? Was he bored being Mr. Mom? Did he want to swing? Was he gay? Was it my fault? What did I do wrong? Almost a decade later, I still don't know the answers. But I have resigned myself to forever being in the dark. I might admit that I am a bit more content about being in the dark today than I was then. Also, what does it fucking matter at this point? A lot of new confusing shit happened in that decade (some of which you're about to read). Time does not heal wounds. Time just distances you from the pain. Only you can heal your own wounds, and only if you want to.

I. Was. Devastated. On the bathroom floor kind of devastated. Not sleeping or eating for months and crying all the time can't breathe kind of devastated. Classic shit.

Then, he married someone else about a year later, so maybe that is what he does? Every seven years, he moves on to the next one? They call this *serial monogamy*. I call it searching for answers in other people when maybe inward is a better place to look.

This began a six-month period that I really don't remember. You see, during that time frame is when my mother and one of my three sisters passed away, both from cancer. To add extra stress, I had just started the new job. It seemed like I was mourning everything and nothing at the same time. Tears would well up in my eyes, without my knowing exactly which thing I was sad about. All I could feel was selfishly desperate and lonely and generally numb.

But I had to keep my shit together at my new job and hold down the fort at home to keep things stable and happy for my daughter. So I shoved all my hideous feelings down deep inside and pretended to be Cleopatra-Queen-of-the-Record-Label at work and Happy-Mommy at home. If I hadn't had my work and home life to keep me on track, I might have been a very special kind of basket case, needing therapy and drugs to find my way back to the light. Before the drama and tragedy overload hit, I had lived a relatively stable and drama-free life, lucky to have my career, friends, family, and true love in my life. Now, with my world upside-down, I was questioning everything. Sadness consumed me, emptiness depressed me, anger hurt me, questions confused me. I was desperate for answers, but no one—least of all my own husband—would provide them. I finally realized I was going to have to find the answers for myself. Within a year, I was slowly walking (more like tip-toeing) a path of self-discovery and recovery.

What helped a little was that the day I (reluctantly) signed the divorce papers, an important album on my record label debuted on the *Billboard* Top 200 chart at #1. Actually, it debuted at #2. But during the twenty-eight minutes I dipped out of work that Wednesday to quickly lend my signature to that piece of paper that made me nauseous (my divorce lawyer's office was conveniently across the street from my office), my record label sales team was furiously disputing the chart numbers and challenging some facts and figures. I went into the divorce lawyer's office a separated woman with a #2 album, and came out a divorced woman with a #1 album. Time to celebrate. I guess.

• • •

After that, several coincidences or signs (sticking finger in throat, I know) led me to the doorstep of the Kabbalah Centre. I was desperate for answers and the Centre was the first place that dared to challenge me to seek and find them myself. In short, Kabbalah offered a logical and practical way of looking at life and its challenges. Studying Kabbalah helped me through these incredibly difficult times and showed me new and productive ways to view the world, problems, situations, interpersonal relationships, religion, and myself. I had reached a major turning point.

Then, I met a guy. He picked me up at a Bon Jovi concert (why I was at a Bon Jovi concert is another story for another time), so smooth and so slick, old-school style. I was very skeptical of his smooth moves at first, but he won me over after a few dates and I accidentally dated him for five years. Ethan was unlike anyone else I had ever been with in many ways: He earned great money as a private doctor with his own practice (I usually went for the starving artist type); he was extremely Jewish (by this I mean on the border of being super religious in an odd, hypocritical way); he was tall, blond, and thick around the middle (*read: kind of fat and I like the skinny/ fit type*); and he smoked weed all day every day (more hypocrisy, since he was a health-care professional). We ate in fine restaurants; traveled the world; laughed; had intellectually stimulating conversations about health, religion, music, politics, and our children. We went to concerts, sporting events, museums. We discussed spending our lives together, but in a void-of-romance way—more like two friends planning a fantasy vacation and discussing logistics.

He asked if I would convert to Judaism—which didn't faze me, since I felt as if I'd already inadvertently converted, thanks to my Kabbalah studies. We went shopping for condos in Florida, where we thought we would eventually retire. He gave me an "engagement" ring. Actually, the way it went down was, he suggested I go get myself a diamond ring. I had a diamond dealer friend named Johnny Rock (real name, no shit) who helped me design and manufacture a beautiful custom sapphire and diamond ring, and then I picked it up with a huge pile of cash Ethan gave me to pay for it. I showed the ring to him one night, very unceremoniously, when I met him outside a Mexican restaurant where we were going to have dinner before seeing Tiesto (not something I would have done on my own, for the record). He said, "Heyyyyyyy, Mazel Tov!" and then the hostess sat us at a table directly next to a girl he had previously dated, who was also going to the concert. He made friendly chit-chat with her, which was fine except that technically we had just gotten "engaged" with the ring I had just given myself using his money.

This was typical of how our relationship unfolded. Nothing really mattered all that much...to either of us, it seemed. Nothing felt significant or momentous. All the talk of love, Judaism, getting married, condo'ing in Florida, would be serious life-changing shit for other couples. For us, it was just conversation, casual ephemeral moments in our lives that never truly merged. We were friends. We had some stuff in common. We both enjoyed a medium-rare filet mignon with peppercorn sauce on the side. That's pretty much what the relationship boiled down to. We both enjoyed various forms of culture and cuisine and had some laughs while he engaged in extravagant spending. I enjoyed our thing, immensely at times, but always with a nagging feeling that this wasn't how love is supposed to be.

The sad truth is, though, I doubted that I would ever have another deep love like I had with my ex-husband. I figured that was a once in a lifetime thing. I believe we call this "settling." All things considered, it wasn't a bad situation to settle for—so I settled. Kind of pitiful.

OK, so, the OTHER truth is, I never truly trusted Ethan. I felt he was shady. I suspected he lied, about many things, big and small. He was often unaccounted for. His phone rang a lot at odd hours. He did a low-talker thing on the phone around me often, and kept his phone face down all the time, which is very suspicious in my opinion. My phone is always face up…which is a little risky, maybe, but I don't really have anything (that much) to hide. What suspicious notifications might be popping up on his phone that required him to keep it face down? Also he was often annoyingly MIA on weekends. He only stayed over at my apartment twice in five years, always using the same excuse about lack of parking. He barely met any of my friends but I met all of his. Life was on his terms.

Although I had keys to his apartment, mostly so that my daughter and I could use the pool on the weekends when he was wherever doing whatever with whomever, he didn't have keys to mine. We led very separate lives. I kept zero clothes or personal items at his house; just a toothbrush that always seemed to be in a different place from where I left it. He didn't even tell me he had a kid for the first eight months of our relationship. It turns out his daughter was born two weeks after our first date.

But once he had come clean about the kid, I thought things would change and all the shadiness would have vanished. It didn't, really. I later discovered that he had a very close relationship with his baby mama. I had assumed they were like an amicable divorced couple who shared custody. Instead, they were "co-parenting," which meant they went on vacations and did shit together that I didn't know about, spending time together as a "family." I think they even had a house upstate together, which explains his weird absences on the weekends. I guess that's what all the low-talking was about.

I wasn't stupid, you know. Nor was I blind. So, what compelled me to stick around in a relationship that was clearly missing big chunks of real-relationship ingredients? I asked myself that question often throughout the five years Ethan and I dated. And, as cynical (and sad) as it sounds, I really didn't believe I could find another true soul mate deep love. Some people never even have one of those at all, so I felt lucky to have had my one-in-a-zillion shot. It had taken me forever to find him in the first place and I even had to import him from Minnesota. So what are the odds I'd find THAT again? Zero point zero.

So I shrugged and went along with what might be a nice substitute for that moment, or maybe even for forever.

Maybe this was serious relationship version 2; Modern Adult Relationship 2.0 that came with a different set of rules that might be tolerable in exchange for its benefits.

I certainly didn't want to move in with Ethan and his spoiled kid. I wanted the freedom to independently reside with my daughter, Imogen (whose name isn't really Imogen, but it's the name that she herself chose for me to use here, which is a testament to her quirky and unique nature). Living with Imogen is like living with a clever comedy writer, whose sense of off-key wit and humor is mature beyond her years. Where *does* she learn all that shit? She is the source of all the joy in my life. I also enjoyed independently managing my demanding career, without having any pressure from a partner all up in my grill. Plus, it was nice to not have to pay for everything myself all the time (story of my life, with my having always dated artistic types) and feel some level of security for the future (both financially and emotionally). I thought I could make this arms-length-relationship-with-commitment thing work for me. The scenario seemed perfect for me at this stage in my life...or it could have been, had there been trust, truth, and loyalty.

Except I didn't trust. He didn't tell the truth. And neither of us was loyal.

Also, I needed to get properly laid on occasion. And that just wasn't Ethan's strong suit. At all. The level of freedom that my long arms gave me made it possible for lots of under-the-radar flings during these five years. I rationalized that my side-dudes were necessary if I wanted to have an orgasm with someone other than myself. At one point, I was even simultaneously dating someone else.

In retrospect, I could have stuck with that guy. He was sweet, loving, normal, sexy, hot, and coincidentally another health-care professional. I called him Hot Male Nurse, which he was, or HMN for short. The only problem with him was that he was seventeen years younger than I was. As you can see, I wasn't sleepwalking through those five years; I spent a lot of the time seeking things to fill a hole, so to speak. Like ordering from an a la carte menu: Boyfriend 1: travel, restaurants, concerts and culture, expensive gifts, and a sense (even if false) of security. Boyfriend 2: hot sex, movies, sleepovers, romance, and hand-holding. Boyfriends 3, 4, 5, 6, ad infinitum: perfect trainer hard bodies, sexy caramel-colored and dark black skin (my weakness and preference, so now you know), and more hot sex. OK, forget "a la carte." It was more like a box of assorted chocolates.

Then, Ethan left me. Big surprise? This time I just rolled with it, though. Like my ex-husband, he never gave me a straight-up reason. He blamed it on the baby mama, his kid, the weather, the direction of the wind. It was all bullshit. Maybe he knew I was cheating but didn't have the balls to come out and say it. And while I was sad to lose my close friend and supposed life partner, (and angry at the immature manner in which it all went down), I knew that I would move on quickly. Deep down I knew that he had been a transitional man, and that the whole thing had been a learning and recovery period for me. I had been well aware of, and purposely ignoring, the abnormality of my settling for a shady hypocrite like Ethan, so I guess I felt an odd sense of relief when I didn't have to keep up the charade.

After all, I had only had two orgasms (with him, that is) in five years. I clearly had a wandering eye (and pussy). And, oh yeah, he called me an N-word-lover in an email. Only he didn't say "N-word," he used the actual N-word. That was the last time we ever communicated.

CHAPTER 2
I'M NOT A SLUT

I'm not a slut. Maybe I exhibit slut-like behavior because I like sex. Does that make me a slut? I also like love—as much as I like sex, if not more.

The truth is, I just want to find the one person who I can have great sex with and also love as a best friend. *The* person. Not multiple people, but *the* person. The person who, the next time I have bad gas and think it's appendicitis and go to the emergency room five days before my best friend's wedding where I am to give an awesome speech and I'm freaking out that I will miss it, will at least text me back to see how I am doing. He doesn't even have to come to the ER in person, maybe just offer to. He would care a little about whether or not I have appendicitis, and maybe meet me for a drink after I am released because I don't.*

I like to think that I am a special breed of woman. Because I'm a little older than the average single bitch and exude a "been there, done that" vibe, my needs may be a bit different from the other ladies searching for the same *Mr. All That & More* that I am. I won't lie, I definitely want all that and more: somebody fit, hot, witty, ten years younger than I, preferably dark, and preferably employed.

But I don't want any more kids. I'm not chasing money. I am entirely self-sufficient. And, I don't even think I want to be married again. Or what might be cool would be to have one of those newfangled marriages where you live separately but are still married, like for health insurance purposes. I'd like a partner, a friend, a sexy fuck buddy, and a lover with jokes and a job, all rolled into one. For life. He would keep me company forever while giving me my precious space. He'd be game to retire somewhere warm…somewhat soon-ish so we can stop working so damn hard.

• • •

My good friend Charles Brown (yes, like Charlie Brown, except my Charlie Brown is a 250-pound dapper black man who wears a blazer with a fancy pocket square that my best friend Chloe mistakenly referred to as an ascot, so now Charlie's nickname is Ascot) says that my special breed is exactly the reason I am "boo-less." He believes that your average guy either wants a subservient woman he can take care of, who validates his masculinity, or just the opposite: a controlling woman (*read: bitch*) who, in effect, replaces his controlling mother (*read: bitch*). While I can mix and match elements from both of those roles, I wouldn't be happy playing either one. Hence, at least according to Ascot, my boo-less state.

I'm pretty clear and specific in my wants, needs, and likes, right? Yet, I still get a lot of unsolicited advice from friends and family about how I ought to compromise certain things. If there is a decent guy around who has to lose some weight or pluck his eyebrows or wax his pubes or wear different sneakers or not tuck that shirt into those pants, I should still date him and work on him later.

This is not for me. I'm not the kind of woman who would control a man like that, no matter how nice a guy he is. I already have a kid I can barely control, so I'm good.

I like a ready-to-wear man. Show up ready for the show, in shape, with your shit together, motherfucker. That's what I am prepared to do, so let's not have different standards. I prefer not to micromanage a man's shortcomings to fit into some mold. If I have to tell him what to wear and to lose twenty pounds, then we don't have that much in common in the first place. It can't be that hard to meet a guy who doesn't need me to tell him that that those jeans are bad and he needs to do crunches and not drink diet soda thinking it's healthy.

We all have our priorities. Mine may be different from yours, but in the end we all want love on our own terms, don't we? Personally, I need to be very physically attracted to a man in order to have sex with him. Luckily, I come across lots of men who I find highly physically attractive, so I have sex with them. That's part of my not-yet-patented, twisted, reverse-courting process; I have sex with someone first, then decide if I like him. The logic seems obvious to me, but I'll state it for the record: Get the fucking out of the way. Was it good or did he show potential? Continue. Wasted a condom? Move on. Does that seem backwards to you? Not to me, as sexual chemistry is of the utmost importance.

"So how long have you been seeing so-and-so?"

"About a month."

"Nice. Did you sleep with him yet?"

"Oh yeah, I slept with him on the first date. We're just getting to know each other now. He's really funny and smart and we are discovering we have so much in common. I think I might like him."

See, in this scenario, the sex can only get better and better as we grow to like each other. So, whose process is more efficient? The traditional 3.2 dates (that's the average, according to a very reliable survey I read on the Internet) followed by unfulfilling, boring, or otherwise unsatisfactory sex on the fourth-ish date seems like a giant waste of everyone's precious time, money, calories, jokes, and oxygen. I maintain that my way is much more efficient.

So in my relentless search for true everlasting love, friendship, and a deep connection, I accidentally behaved like a slut.

For the record, I am not a hypochondriac who rushes to the ER for a paper cut. My next-door neighbor who is a nurse urged me to go to the twenty-four-hour walk-in clinic where the doctor on call examined me and told me to go straight to the emergency room because I had clear symptoms of appendicitis. This did actually happen and the boyfriend at the time (Mr. HH, you'll meet him soon) texted me back about five hours later, after I had already been released. Thanks anyway.

CHAPTER 3

C-LO & DEL TACO

Everyone needs a best friend to whom she can spill all her inner horror. I met Chloe through work during the time I was happily (?) married and she was happily (?) in a relationship with her live-in boyfriend of ten-plus years. Ours is a long distance friendship—she lives in LA—but we still consider ourselves to be best friends. As best friends often do, we live strangely parallel lives. We have had similar work drama, similar health issues, and general life resemblances. And when my marriage abruptly ended, coincidentally, so did her relationship. These corresponding events made us even closer friends as we compared notes on the horrors of heartbreak, betrayal, and desperate sadness, all while holding down our successful careers and cheering each other on.

Because of the distance, we communicated mainly by email, the best way for two creative types to type, think, write, joke, and spill it all. It's like writing in a diary, only with someone actually on the other side to read your words, laugh at you, and cry along with you... and maybe even provide some advice, for better or worse.

I wasn't sure if I was emailing Chloe for her advice, for shock value, or just to vent. Mostly, I wanted to make her laugh at the absurdity of what my life had turned into after my marriage ended and I found myself confused and searching for love and happiness Round Two, not knowing where it might be hiding or how to get there. My emails to C-Lo (like J-Lo or CeeLo before they were "J-Lo" and "CeeLo") were raw, honest, and soul-baring, but also so ridiculous and ludicrous. One of my emails prompted her to say, "I'm going to start a blog with all your emails, your shit is crazy."

I've decided to include some of the emails here verbatim. For starters, you'll learn some of the code names we devised for all the guys who came in and out of my life, like HMN for Hot Male Nurse, and MD, our nickname for Ethan. It didn't stand for Medical Doctor, as you might think, but for Major Dick. Is it bad if you think your boyfriend is a dick?

Email to Chloe, about a year into relationship with MD:
Get a load of this shit. MD and I were out to a fancy dinner last night so I was a little dressed up and I wanted to stay out. So we went for drinks at some club on the west side where I always wanted to go based on its...um... diversity. While he was ordering drinks at the bar, I went to the bathroom. There was a hot young black guy in line and when I asked him if this was the bathroom line, he turned around, eyed me up and down, smiled a giant big white grin and said "Well, look at you!" He chatted me up the entire bathroom line time. It was a co-ed bathroom, so once we got inside, we used

adjoining stalls. **After we were both finished, while hand-washing and lipstick-applying, we exchanged phone numbers and he took a selfie of us in the mirror as he proclaimed, "What a gorgeous couple we make!" I told him I had to go, and I think he knew what I meant.**

He texted me already this morning and we're going out later this week. He's a nurse, like a serious male nurse in a cancer-care ward at a major hospital. That shit is no joke. I am afraid, however, he is like half my age, but OMG so hot and cute. Hot Male Nurse.

I actually dated HMN on the regular. This is odd behavior, I know, I admit. But as I said earlier in my own defense, I was just trying to fill in some empty spots. I didn't have the balls to break it off with MD because there were lots of benefits to that relationship that I selfishly didn't want to give up. Also, I'm weak. I just couldn't resist the charm and allure of this young, sweet, sexy Hot Male Nurse who didn't care about our Demi Moore/Ashton Kutcher age difference. He thought I was hot and wanted to be with me. Who could resist that?

So, yeah, I was shady, too. But deep-down inside, I truly didn't want to be shady. I only wanted to be loved completely and I felt only partially liked in both situations. The combination of the two guys was meant to fulfill me, but of course it didn't. I eventually decided that HMN would make someone a terrific boyfriend, but sadly, that wasn't going to be me. I had also finally reached the end of my rope with MD, and with C-Lo's help, decided to bust the break-up move on him.

But before I could actually execute that plan, I had to take a business trip to LA. I was looking forward to hanging out with C-Lo while I was there, so we could discuss my break-up plan of action in person. When I logged on to American Airlines' website to check in for my flight, my computer's "keychain" had MD's frequent flyer number and password saved from the last visit, when MD had logged on using my computer. It took me a second to realize that I wasn't actually looking at my reservation, but that of a Rachel Kahn, from Miami to Newark a week from now, on MD's account; she was arriving on a Tuesday evening, departing early the next day. A flight for a girl from Miami for just one night.

Now, that was interesting. My first thought was, why does he have to fly a Jewish girl up from Miami to have a fling? He can't find someone local? I sat on this information for a minute. Of course I had no right to be accusatory, so I needed to decide how to handle it. For some reason, I chose to text him from my gate at the airport with a simple, "Who is Rachel Kahn?"

MD: A friend of my cousin's from Miami. Why?
MM: So is she coming to visit you?
MD: Why are you asking this?
MM: Well, I happened to log in to your airline account and I see that you're flying her up for the night next month.
MD: Why did you log in to my account?
MM: It was an autofill on my computer when I

went to check in for my flight today. Totally unintentional. Imagine my surprise.

At this point, my flight was boarding.

    MD: She's cool, she's a friend of my cousin.

    MM: So, is she staying with you?

    MD: Nooooooooo, I'm not even going to see her. I just got her a flight as a favor for my cousin.

    MM: Sounds like more of a favor for Rachel.

Group 2 is now boarding. Fuck.

    MM: I'm getting on the plane. So, what's the story?

Nothing. I had to board that plane while waiting for a reply. Waiting and waiting and waiting until the very last possible moment to shut down. Even past the very last moment because I didn't actually turn the phone off until after take-off. Nothing.

I felt ill the whole flight. Sweaty palms and that sick feeling in my stomach. Considering that I wasn't completely invested in the relationship with MD, and was actually planning to end it, this feeling came as a surprise. What was it? I had six long hours to identify it. Jealousy, anger, hurt, surprise, curiosity—as in, is he really playing me to this extent?—all went through my head. *So…this has to be it, right? This is clearly the final straw. So why do I still feel so ill about it?*

When the flight landed, six fucking hours later, and I still had no response from MD, I called him. And got no answer, of course. So I texted, "Landed. Give me a call when you can talk."

Chloe picked me up at the airport and immediately sensed weird-vibe when I got in the car.

"What? No hug?"

"Oh I'm sorry, ma, I am so happy to see you! Listen to this shit..."

As she drove us to her house, she listened to me ramble on and on about the situation and all of its possibilities and repercussions. Somewhere on La Cienega Boulevard, MD called back.

"FUCK. IT'S HIM," I screamed. "I have to deal with this. Don't listen in and try to make me laugh!"

Chloe decided it was important to give me privacy so she pulled the car into the parking lot of a Del Taco and got out. She paced and smoked her weekly cigarette (she just couldn't totally abandon them quite yet), while I sat curbside and listened to this oddly believable story. Apparently Rachel Kahn, a close friend of MD's cousin from Miami, was a single mom and a devout Jew. There is some gravesite in Queens where a particular rabbi is buried and devotees go there to say prayers and leave handwritten letters expressing their desires. MD's "mitzvah" was to pay for this woman's flight to NYC so she could visit the gravesite and say her prayer, as she had always wanted to do it but couldn't afford the trip. She was a single mom, hence the quick overnight turnaround.

This was actually plausible, but it still seemed shady as fuck and I was very suspect of it. The Del Taco conversation would not be easily dismissed or forgotten. I noted the date of her trip on my calendar so I could monitor where MD was that night. In fact, because I had aborted the break-up plan when all those jealous feelings were flying around, we ended up having dinner on that very date and I stayed over at his place. So maybe the story was true. Or maybe she had canceled her trip. Or maybe she had postponed it. Or maybe it just doesn't fucking matter.

Email to Chloe about a month later:

Jesus fucking Christ, how long can this go on? I'm sick of this uncertainty about MD. I'm sick of his disappearing acts and suspect behavior. You can't play a playa. I think it's finally time to stop this charade, it's just not worth it. I'm not saying HMN is the answer, but I think I need to eliminate MD once and for all. I can't be Del Taco'ing anymore; it's too exhausting. We are having dinner tomorrow night and I think I need to just end it. Break it off for good. Give me strength, girl!

Chloe talked to me on the phone the whole time I drove to Brooklyn to meet MD for dinner. She gave me strength and courage and reminded me that I deserved better. She gave me a few suggestions on what to say and how to say it and wished me luck. "You can do it, you slut!"

Dinner was super awkward, obviously. I worked up my courage and waited until the wine was poured to bring up the topic of our relationship. Smooth-Move-MD, however, quickly picked up on where I was heading and turned the conversation right around. He slickly stopped me dead in my tracks by complimenting me, raving about our relationship, talking about future stuff, and navigating around the topic of exclusivity.

"So, let me ask you something," he said. "Who was the guy I saw you making out with in front of your building?"

"What? What guy? I wasn't making out with anyone in front of my building."

This is true. I don't make out with guys in front of my building. I did, however, remember hugging HMN good night one recent evening. I hadn't let him come upstairs because I had determined that this was the beginning of the end for both HMN and MD. I also remembered having a drink date with a guy from work. That one happened to turn into a little bit more, but not too much more because I very intentionally said goodnight to him in front of my building rather than inside my apartment. So, as I was trying to figure out which semi- innocent incident MD might be referring to, he continued.

"Yeah you were. I saw you making out with someone and it made me sick."

"What were you doing outside my building?"

"I was just driving by."

"Oh, you just happened to be driving by my apartment at night? Well, I'm sure I wasn't making out with anyone."

"Well I know what I saw, and I saw you with another man outside your building. I never said anything about it because I didn't want to even think about you sleeping with other guys. But I know what I saw."

I considered this. "Well I obviously wasn't sleeping with whoever it was if I was saying goodnight outside of my building instead of going upstairs."

At that point, I remembered my original intention for this conversation and decided to go balls deep. "So. Was he black or white?"

• • •

I was unsuccessful in breaking up with MD that night. Somehow, he magically turned everything around so that I felt like the pot calling the kettle black (OK, not the best analogy here, I realize). And while he was flying the mysterious Rachel Kahn to NYC, his charming self was also spending time with me the very night she was supposed to be here. Plus, he was clearly willing to look the other way after witnessing my semi-indiscretion first-hand. I did feel for MD deeply enough to have all those sick jealous feelings when I discovered that airline ticket. He was definitely a more viable option for long-term security and steadiness and more age-appropriate than HMN, so I decided I wanted to try again.

I kept an eye on that American Airlines account and saw minimal suspicious activity. (I didn't consider the by-now routine family vacations with the baby mama "suspicious" at this point. If he wasn't fucking her, what did I care? And even if he was, that's just gross and not my problem).

So we moved on, together. Sort of. Either his secrecy was lessening or I was becoming more tolerant of it. There were still a lot of low-talking phone conversations, I never saw him on weekends, and his baby mama was overly reliant on him to the point where I still felt as if I was last on his list of priorities:

1. His kid (no brainer)
2. His baby mama (weird)
3. Work (OK, I might give in on this one)
4. (or maybe tied for #1) Weed
5. (and last) Me.

Another woman's name regularly popped up on his phone (when it wasn't facedown). He said she was a work acquaintance, but who calls a work acquaintance at both 8:00 a.m. and 11:00 p.m. and at all hours in between? I saw this woman's name on the American Airlines account too, but the flight was from New York to somewhere in California, with another ticket for a woman who shared her same last name. I assumed this was another mitzvah for a mother/daughter or maybe two sisters. I didn't even bother to ask. I don't think I cared enough to, and also didn't want to get busted for regularly checking MD's airline account. But obviously the shadiness endured.

• • •

Email to Chloe:
> In other news, I just got a big giant bouquet of roses from MD delivered to my office. He knows that I am super annoyed at his behavior yesterday because he canceled plans that we had made ages ago. I got myself on the guest list to see my favorite band of all time, Earth, Wind & Fire, knowing full well that he was just humoring me by agreeing to go. Well he

fucking canceled at the last minute with some bullshit excuse about baby mama needing to work late, so he had to be with his kid but I am skeptical about this being the truth. I had to scramble to find someone to go with, but luckily everyone LOVES them some EWF, so I went with Ascot and we had a blast of course. Anyway, MD's card with the goddamn flowers just said, "I love you." Well I love him too, but I am also hot for the trainer, whom I do not love.

Every one of these trainers is so fucking hot. The trainers at my gym are enough to cast a hot male review troupe, or a porn flick. Seriously, I was like a dog in heat on any given day. I hadn't been properly laid in a really long time, so that may have affected my judgment about what is hot and what is not. I recognized that not being properly laid was my own doing...I recognized this to be a major rut.

I go to the gym just about every morning, in between dropping off Imogen at school and going to work. That's been my stay-fit routine for as long as I have had a daughter to drop off. I don't treat the gym as if it's a nightclub, like some do—that's just a bonus. It would be part of my daily life, lucky me, even without the bonuses and benefits.

HDT (Hot Dominican Trainer), the "bang" we kicked off with, was my recurring special indulgence. Apart from our first encounter, when we had lunch first, we never did anything but have sex in my bed on occasional afternoons or evenings. Maybe if I hadn't been with MD at the time, there would have been more. He did invite me to come to his apartment once and might even have mentioned the obligatory movie. And he spent time with me at the gym, giving me tips, stretching me, helping me with whatever injury or aches and pains I may have had. I knew his schedule and sometimes I purposely planned to work out when I knew he would be there. Other times, when I didn't feel my best or just wasn't in the mood for all that heavy flirting, I went to a different gym location. HDT was a beautifully fine man, a caramel-colored Dominican whose body was perfect in every way, as I mentioned, and a sweet soul and a caring lover. Brains... not so much.

I sent Chloe a photo of HDT.
>**Chloe: That's a crazy ill body!!!!**
>**Me: You're lucky I didn't send you the ones of his giant hard cock.**

I also regularly flirted with HCT, Hot Cuban Trainer. We exchanged phone numbers, we went cycling together one weekend, which I thought might develop into something, but it only led to a sweaty-post-bike-ride make-out session and nothing further. We still flirted, suggesting that there may be unfinished business, but we never did finish.

There were others whom I admired from afar: Deon, Clarence, the one with the African name that I forget, another Dominican, a Trinidadian...assorted eye candy everywhere!

And there was the Crown Jewel of all trainers. Of all men, even. I had my eye on this guy since what felt like the dawn of time, beginning while I was still married. Ours was a strong, ancient attraction that began with our original souls fucking each other prior to the Big Bang (no pun intended) that formed the solar system. That had to be it, because it was just about the most intense physical attraction to another human being I have ever felt, right up there with that chemistry I felt with my ex-husband.

One evening, early in Year One of being a divorcee, I went to the local elementary school to pick up Imogen from her after school program that took place in the gym. Just outside the gym entrance, among all the working parents rushing to pick up their kids, there was a congregation of tall, athletic, fit, chocolate special treats. I thought to myself, "WHERE HAVE ALL *THESE* DADS BEEN?!!!" I said as much to one of my close mom friends who replied, "You idiot, those guys play basketball in the gym every Monday at 6."

Oh.

But I *know* that one. That's *the one* from the gym. Oh thank you, thank you, universe! I was able to catch his eye and sexy killer smile and we had a quick flirty chat about basketball on Mondays, my daughter attending school there and, wouldn't it be cute if he taught my daughter how to play basketball one day? It was an especially magical flirtation as it was off gym property and on neutral territory. From then on, I always wore something especially interesting or sexy or stylish to work on Mondays, and on my way to the school from my office, I fixed my hair, applied lipstick, and moved that blood diamond ring to the other finger.

Our attraction went beyond the banal nature of his hot trainer body and my horny cougar ways. There was something about this man that drew me in, as if he'd cast a supernatural spell on me. The last time I'd felt like this was about my husband, before he was my husband, while he was somebody else's husband and well before he was my ex-husband. And this soul-fucking trainer actually was someone else's husband, so, to protect the innocent as well as the guilty, I will leave it at that. But, before you judge me (if it's not too late for that), let's take a moment to quote the progressive feminist heroine Helen Gurley Brown, who said, "To me, avoiding married men totally when you're single would be like passing up first aid in a Tijuana hospital when you're bleeding to death because you prefer an immaculate American hospital some unreachable distance across the border."

Exactly, lady. If I had previously avoided married men, I never would have had seven glorious years of marriage and a beautiful daughter. Yes, I know. No need to remind me of the soul-crushing heartbreak, drama, and devastation, but that's not the point right now.

Email to Chloe:

My Kabbalah teacher told me that November is a crazy fucking month and that we encounter all kinds of problems and challenges, one after the other, nonstop. But one of the ways to overcome those obstacles and lessen their severity is to examine yourself and figure out something you need to LET GO of. So. I thought about it…and

I'm LETTING GO of the idea that I want to fuck hot trainers every day.

Think I can do it???

Well, you might like to know that I did do it. For a bit. I was faithful to MD.

CHAPTER 4
OFFICE PARTY

Email to Chloe:

Sit down and don't multitask while you read this email. MD had his office holiday party last week. He hosted dinner for a bunch of rowdy doctors and their office assistants. None of these people get out much (unlike MD), so they all overdid it. They went to Sammy's Romanian in the East Village, where they serve you entire bottles of vodka with your dinner. As if that wasn't enough drinking, afterwards the whole crew went to The Bowery Ballroom to see Matisyahu. One of the drunken doctors was buying shots of tequila for everyone there...you can only imagine how insane the night got after that point.

Someone lost his wallet, someone else threw up outside, yet another person got lost on the way home. MD also had his issues. He took a cab to where he thought his car was parked but then remembered he didn't drive. So he took another cab to the train station to go to Brooklyn and remembered that his keys were in another guy's car. He finally made it home, totally wasted, disheveled, bruised, and scratched. Once he was safe in bed, at 1am-ish, that's when the drunk-texts started. Here they are exactly as they appeared with some minor editing.

MD: Have you lied to me? About other men? Because I really love you.

MM: ?? Where is this coming from?

MD: It makes me ill to think of you and other men. I'm drunk and extremely jealous.

MM: Why on earth would you think that? You're my man and I love you.

MD: I'm drunk. Ignore me.

(Which I should have done exactly at this moment)

MM: OK, sleep it off.

MD: I love you spoooofuckem much.

MM: I love you too. And I am happy to remind you that I am wearing your bling on my finger.

MD: I never want anyone but you. You broke my heart when I saw you take someone else upstairs.

MM: I'm a little worried. Are you OK? Why would you be having these thoughts?

MD: I'm trippin.

MD: You brok my heart when I drov by your place, I dn't care Nymorep

MM: Why bring that up now? That's ancient history.

(More of this same shit)

> MD: I'm extremely jealousy. And that night I drove by ANd saw you wit someone else it made me ill. Destroyed me to see you kissing soemone else.

(pause)

> MD: I thought we were together and then I saw you take somenigger home.
> MM: Ancient history. Please stop.
> MD: Is my dick not big enough?
> MM: Seriously?
> MD: I hate the fact that you selpt with sopme nigger when we were suppoposed to be together.

So there it is. That's the answer to the burning question from over 2 years ago: "Was he black or white?"

The next day, big apologies came flooding in around noon.

> MD: I really can't believe that I have such an amazing woman in my life and in the back corner of my mind I think stupid shit. I don't think any of that stuff that I texted you, I was drinking Insecure Vodka.

Oh, the guilt. I'm such an asshole. I think the trainers and the HMNs and the various boy toys are really truly going to have to be ancient history now.

CHAPTER 5

ONCE MORE WITH (LESS) FEELING!

What do normal people do on the weekends? Every other weekend and a day or two each week, Imogen stays with her father—thus enabling me to engage in aforementioned shenanigans. During those times, I feel like I should be taking advantage of her absence by swinging from the chandeliers. Or, doing cultured New Yorker-type things like going to the Guggenheim by myself to absorb something I think I'm interested in (but really, I can't tolerate the crowds so I'd get annoyed and end up buying some useless Frank Lloyd Wright souvenir such as a Guggenheim-shaped cookie jar in the gift shop to reward myself for even trying). Or taking advantage of a beautiful day and jogging four miles, then stopping off at the farmer's market for some organic green shit to cook up and eat on my terrace (if I had one) while reading someone's scintillating memoir (who is far more interesting and funnier than I). Or, better yet, spending time with my fucking boyfriend.

Oh, right, he's off in New Paltz or at his "aunt's house" in the Hamptons or somewhere with his ghost family and therefore unavailable to me.

I'd try to make brunch, drinks, or dinner dates with girlfriends, work friends, the gays, but alas no one was ever free on the weekends because they all have other important shit to do with their own families and significant others.

Sometimes I would actually swing from the chandeliers with an HDT or HMN, but mostly I didn't do much of anything other than run errands, go to the gym, take a nap, and maybe binge-watch cable shows at top volume that have a lot of cursing in them that I don't watch while Imogen is home. (To be clear, nothing outside of G-rated behavior happens while Imogen is home, like I live two lives.) Then I'd feel like having a glass of wine, but I am not an alone-drinker. As much as I would love to be able to enjoy a glass of wine and relax by myself, I end up feeling tipsy after half a glass and start talking to myself and then falling asleep on the couch. So instead, I'd stick my head out my apartment door and see if there was any action next door.

My next-door neighbor of fifteen years, Louise, was a bright, energetic, fit, stylish, warm, and loving woman of seventy years who was like family to me. Our doors were adjacent in the pre-War Manhattan building we shared. Sometimes it seemed as if we were more like roommates than neighbors; we had keys to each other's apartments and checked with each other before going to the store— "Need anything?"

There is an intimacy in small Manhattan buildings that others might not understand. Ours was like a commune, and Louise was its leader and the host of all the parties. And by all the parties, I mean ALL the parties.

The consummate New Yorker, she had synagogue friends (she had her Bat Mitzvah at age sixty-five, affirming that it's never too late for anything), wine club friends, theater-going friends, upstate friends, antique dealer friends, and the gays with whom she took spin class twice a week. Practically every day of the week, there was a different group of eclectic folks drinking in apartment 2B.

While she was a warm, loving, and selfless woman, Louise was also like a bossy Jewish aunt who made you feel guilty for not checking in often. She had that authoritative-elder quality that simply had to be dutifully obeyed. One year, when we were each planning our own separate Thanksgiving celebrations with family and friends, she declared that we would create a double-apartment Thanksgiving combo party by propping both apartment doors open and utilizing both kitchens and ovens. Her apartment would be for appetizers and the main course, mine for the bar, dessert and coffee. This was such a success that we employed the tactic for multiple holidays. I loved living next door to her.

One fall, Louise fell ill with what she thought was pneumonia. She avoided seeing me and Imogen because she had lost so much weight and she didn't want us to worry. I stayed away and gave her privacy on instinct. She'd said she was still planning a trip to Russia with her travel buddies as soon as she recovered, so I figured I'd hear from her when that time came. But instead, at 6:00 a.m. on a cold February Sunday morning, I got a frantic call from her best friend.

I'd had no idea Louise's illness was that bad. I raced to the hospital with another neighbor from my building who was equally surprised. We each were able to spend some time with at her bedside and, although she was unconscious, I scolded her for hiding from me for so many months. My last words to dear Louise were something like, "You know, I'm kinda mad at you," but truthfully I think she would have laughed and said, "Well, fuck you, too," or something equally snarky.

More friends started to show up to the hospital; the synagogue friends, the family friends, the traveling buddies, the neighbors, the relatives, the spin class. The waiting area at New York Presbyterian hospital had never seen such a crowd. We were a huge mob that spilled out into the hallway because there were not enough seats for everyone. We were noisy. We chatted, caught up with each other, told stories, argued, yelled, cried, and hugged. Typical Louise; she drew a diverse crowd of friends together from all aspects of her life even from her unconscious state. As the winter sun set early, little by little the mob dissipated off into the cold and we peeled off to go our separate ways. I think she waited until most everyone was gone. That was Louise's last party.

Family, friends, and neighbors sat *shiva* in her apartment, using mine for the spillover. It was like so many other parties we had hosted that it felt as if Louise would walk in any moment, directing us as to which plates to use for serving, where to put the ice bucket and glasses for drinks, and which knives went with which cheeses. We knew never, ever to serve on paper plates, as this was Louise's rule. For the whole week, the doors were propped open and people constantly came and went, and Louise's dog was confused. It was a whirlwind of sadness and celebration, and I, unfortunately, had some experience on this roller coaster ride of extreme feelings, as did my daughter, even at her tender age of ten.

• • •

I wondered when MD would stop by for *shiva*. He was well aware that I had my hands full, so I assumed he was allowing me the space and time I needed and would stop by toward the end of the week to pay his respects. But he didn't. Then, everyone was gone.

Things had quieted down but there remained so many questions about what would happen next. *Shiva* may have been over and the (literal and figurative) door closed, but the wrapping up of Louise's amazing life was just about to begin. Because I had been (literally and figuratively) close to her, I knew that I would play some small part in the process, along with her family members. As I considered what my role might be, I tried to resume my daily routine with Imogen. The sooner things got back to normal with us, the better it would be for her, regardless of how unsettled I was still feeling.

One evening, I was making dinner while my smart, nerdy girl was doing her homework when MD called. He sounded weird. I was ready to forgive him for not coming by to pay his respects, but he interrupted by saying, "We have to change things…with our relationship."

I was unaware that MD was breaking up with me at this very moment because:

a. I was in the middle of preparing dinner;
b. I was fresh from the burial of my dear friend, so nothing made a whole lot of sense;
c. He was not 100 percent clear in his communication, not offering any specifics but instead some rhetoric about "making changes"; and
d. The "changes" were related to the usual nonsensical, shady bullshit with the baby mama and something about them having another baby so his kid could have a sibling.

Once I caught the drift, I hung up on him—because I couldn't believe that, after five years, he'd chosen to go with a phone break-up while I was cooking dinner, right after my friend died. Never mind the fact that he actually wanted another baby with a woman he was not in love with. This was not the right moment for me to delve into the finer points of his argument—or even try to wrap my head around what he was trying to say.

Subsequently, there were a few more semi-cohesive attempts at communication on his part, via email and texts, but there was never another call or face-to-face encounter. The texts and emails were confusing, but somewhere in between the lines there were cloudy attempts at maintaining a friendship, possibly even a reconciliation. He suggested we meet for a "sandwich." But when my replies challenged him to explain himself further, his tone changed and his language became peppered with insults and accusations. Finally, at Chloe's urging, I asked him to stop contacting me entirely; I told him that if and when I was ready to be friends with him, I'd be in touch. He replied with something like this:

Stop acting like a bitch. I don't need a N*gger lover being in my life.

When you've gone that far, why even bother with that asterisk, is my question.

Delete.

I never heard from him again.

• • •

It was plainly obvious that my relationship with MD would eventually come to an end. The circumstances around its final demise, however, were eerily similar to those at the end of my marriage. Death comes in threes: friend, relationship, job. Why is that, though? There must be some kind of pattern or cosmic reason. So if you're some kind of psychologist or psychic or if you have any sort of insight as to why this repeat pattern happens, could you please get in contact with me and let me know your theories? I'd appreciate it because I'm still trying to work it out myself.

The Kabbalists believe that when a death occurs, the soul still lives on; that death is only an illusion. But what is illusory about something you care about flat out disappearing from your daily life? Does it disappear—or does your relationship with it simply change?

Once again, I found myself grieving multiple deaths. It was like a seven-year cycle: relationship death (MD), family member death (Louise), job death (record label where I worked for seven years was dissolving). But, on a more positive note, it was also a seven-year cycle of multiple beginnings: relationship beginning (time to find what I really want and deserve), family member beginning (time to move on from the past and to welcome a new neighbor), job beginning (time to accept an opportunity to join a start-up record label).

By this point, I understood that life can change quickly and suddenly at any moment, and that when those sudden shifts happen, priorities fall into perspective. What was important to me at that moment? Coming to terms with losing Louise. Concentrating on the well-being of my daughter. Solidifying my next career move. Maybe that's the cosmic answer to why death happens in threes. The universe says, "RESET, BITCH."

I knew that grieving for a relationship in which I was not perfectly happy would not do me any good. I had given the relationship the respect it deserved by recognizing and feeling my sadness that it ended. Having been through it all before, I decided that this time it would be once more...with less feeling.

• • •

I enjoy my alone time when Imogen is not home; I like my space and freedom. I also cherish our time together as mother and daughter. As she has matured, her sense of humor has developed into a sophisticated kind of high comedy. Sometimes, I feel as if she fills the best friend void that her father left. But there is still something missing. When I have no significant other, I feel lonely.

Friends and family can only go so far in that area, but thank you for your offer and best efforts. When I'd whine about needing a man, I'd get some pep talk like Ascot's "new ass is the best remedy for old ass, go find a trainer to fuck" or C-Lo's "fuck him, he just doesn't know how awesome you are" or my cousin's "he is immature, let him go." None of this helps me in the least, but thank you anyway. I like a steady man in my life. Who doesn't?

They (whoever *they* are) say that when you want to find someone, you should *not* actively look. Not looking is how you find someone. Stop looking and this person just miraculously shows up. How does that make sense? Please explain.

A whole different *they* says that you have to get off your ass and get out there and turn over every stone and go on every date and "put it out there" to everyone who crosses your path that you're aggressively looking for a mate. This is possibly just as illogical and also sounds exhausting.

As much action as I would have in the next couple of months with the help of a variety of trainers and HMNs, I knew these were fleeting moments of satisfaction that would not lead me to a permanent solution. So I decided to go ahead and "put it out there."

CHAPTER 6

AMTRAK, RED WINE, & ANAL SEX

Email to Chloe:

Do all men want anal sex? What IS that? It's like all the rage now. Men are all confident and cocky, asking for and even demanding anal sex. It's all MD ever talked about. I don't get it. Is it a thing now? I never had to deal with this so much before, what gives?

Charlie Brown told me that all men want anal sex. He thinks it's just a fact. I still don't believe this to be true, but it was relevant because I was single and dating. It's a non-starter for me personally, but it's interesting to hear different perspectives. I certainly wanted to be prepared to address the topic early in an intimate relationship so that there would be no confusion or false hope.

I met a guy on Match.com. I figured out that online dating is just what you do today instead of picking up people in a bar (or the gym, in my case), which is a shame considering that I've become something of a professional after all my years of experience and success. But online dating does make more sense. Between conversing with a total stranger at a club based purely on his physical appearance and choosing to test drive someone based on a myriad of pre-determined common interests, online dating has better odds than the traditional hooker-style to which I was accustomed. But Match.com may not have been the right website for me. Despite the fact that I filled out a detailed profile indicating my preference for tall, fit men of African American descent (I'd rather just say "black," if that's OK), who are marginally educated, who drink socially and don't smoke, it was the short, fat, balding white guys photographed with their mid-life crisis motorcycles who reached out to me.

I was waiting around for something to magically happen. When it didn't, I made the bold decision to reach out to a few guys instead. I found one handsome black guy who had about twenty-seven photos of himself on his profile. I figured all those photos meant he was being honest and presenting himself in a true light, dispelling any doubts or possibility for misrepresentation. He looked consistently attractive in all the photos taken in various settings and attire from business suit to beach wear. In one of the twenty-seven photos, he was wearing a pink blazer. "That's got to be a secure man who wears a pink blazer," I thought. So I "liked" the photo. No response. But I did have a few exchanges with some other interesting-looking men. One very suave gentleman in a suit, posing next to his fancy car, emailed me that he believed we were "perfect for each other" based on our profiles. That very well may have been true, but I guess neither of us will ever know since he never responded to my email asking to hear more about him.

Then I met a police sergeant with the screen name *GoMets,* whose profile emphasized (redundantly) that he was an avid sports fan. He was sweet, ready to dive headfirst into a relationship and be a stepdad, but because he revealed all of this within the first seventeen minutes of our drinks date, I was not so sure that's what I wanted. He also didn't appear to have any interests outside of guy stuff like bein' a cop, watchin' sports, eatin' barbeque, and livin' in Queens, near where the Mets play.

I had another drink date with yet another police officer who very quickly revealed his foot fetish. I decided to give the site a rest. Maybe the right guy for me just hadn't signed up yet.

• • •

A few weeks later, one lonely night, I went trolling for black guys on Match.com again. I saw a handsome-looking guy who had posted about twenty-seven photos of himself, including one in which he was wearing a pink blazer, and I thought, "That must be a secure man who can wear a pink blazer," so I "liked" the photo.

Wait. Didn't I already see this photo? Didn't I email with this guy already?

This time, I received an email from him that same night, introducing himself as Dele (pronounced DAY-LAY) and asking me out for a drink, "how's tomorrow?"

TOMORROW??

"Yes, tomorrow. Why waste time?"

OK, great, I like the way this guy thinks. We're not getting any younger.

It wasn't the greatest first date ever, but it certainly wasn't the worst. In fact, there were lots of positives about it. First off, he was willing to come to my neighborhood and asked me to choose a place. I gave him three options, and he picked my favorite one. When I walked in, he stood up, hugged me, and held a chair out for me. He immediately said, "Your photos don't do you justice," which was a lovely compliment. He looked exactly like his twenty-seven photos. We made polite conversation during which I discovered he was from Nigeria, which is a whole different flavor brother. A glass of wine into it, we were chatting away like old friends. Another glass of wine and we decided to have some food. I can't remember how much more wine there was after that, but I do know that if I hadn't had to go home to relieve the babysitter, there would have been more wine and who knows what else.

On our second date, there was a nice brain connection on top of the initial attraction. I felt comfortable talking to him, though I did feel a slight disconnect when discussing our careers. Ever try to talk to a Wall Street banker about an idea you have for a music video? He seemed to see my music business career as a nice little hobby, while his big broker job (or whatever) was crucially important to the world as we know it.

As we became acquainted, I was unsure what to think. I was still assessing. He seemed chivalrous. He was appropriately silly and made me laugh. And, he was honest. Maybe too honest. When we were comparing notes about previous relationships, he told me a story about a woman he'd gone out with and why he ended things. As he told it, when they became intimate, he noticed a really foul odor. He suspected it was coming from her vagina, so he did a move where he started to finger her, then maneuvered his body position so that he could surreptitiously sniff his finger. As he'd suspected, the odor on his finger was so foul that immediately lost his erection and slowly extricated himself from the situation. He excused himself by saying that he was really tired and had to go, and thanked her for a great night.

According to the story, he never called her again, but she relentlessly pursued him. I'm sure she was confused by the abrupt stoppage. After avoiding her calls and texts questioning him about why he just disappeared, Dele finally decided to be a big man about it. He called her back and told her the truth. It was nothing that she had said or done, he explained. It was the horrible smell emanating from her pussy. She called him a fucking asshole and hung up on him.

Now, I still can't decide what his truth-telling says about his character. Was that a stand-up guy thing to do, or should he have just politely made up some other excuse? Somehow, I kind of feel like he did the right thing. But it's hard to say if this was an asshole move or not.

Dele and I had sex on the third date. I made sure my pussy was clean. I came more times in three hours than I did in five years with MD. I am still not sure if the pussy-licking was all that great, or if I had been on a desert island for five years and someone showed up with a hamburger and a milkshake (which, under normal, not-starving circumstances is not something I would eat). Regardless, it worked for me, and continued to do so on a regular basis. Until the rest of it didn't.

During the three months I dated Dele, there were plenty of deafeningly loud warning bells, but I guess I felt like putting my fingers in my ears and yelling "la la la la la" instead of heeding them. I was just so excited to be in a pseudo-relationship with a brain housed in a hot body that wanted to hang out in my apartment and make me come on a regular basis. But in retrospect, the red flags were there:

Our first kiss: It was on that first date. He was in the middle of chewing a meatball appetizer when he kissed me as I got up to use the ladies room.

Our Second Date: After our second date, we were making out in his car and he said, "I want you to be my woman," which was exciting at the time, but in retrospect, it was too soon and he kind of just wanted to own me, like how you own a golden retriever.

Names: He didn't believe my age, and playfully demanded to see my driver's license. Maybe this was a textbook move from the "Online Dating Safety Tips" handbook, but after I proved how ancient I was, I asked to see his license, too. I saw that his full first native Nigerian name was Oladele. "Oh, what fun, I can call you 'Oladele' now, your *real* name." He vehemently refused to acknowledge me if I ever referred to him by his proper name—and this was without any trace of playfulness. At one point, he told me about his best friend from Nigeria, Steve, and when I asked what Steve's real name was, he assured me it was *Steve*. I had a feeling no one in Nigeria was calling their sons *Steve* at birth so I pushed the issue. Being genuinely curious about culture and tradition, and as a world traveler and student of life that I am, I wanted to know Steve's real name.

"Have you ever been to Nigeria?" he challenged.

"No," I admitted.

"Well then how do you know people there aren't called Steve?"

"Well, I don't *know*, but I thought he might have a traditional name, like yours. Why can't you just tell me his name?"

I really wanted to know.

His answer was, "If you ever meet Steve, you can ask him his real name yourself."

General demeanor: He was rude to hostesses, waiters, and waitresses, which is a general red flag for me, indicating a person who has no humanity.

His Attire: Maybe ridiculous jackets were his trademark; remember the pink one? One night, I was having a pre-drink at our meeting place with Charlie Brown aka Ascot, who looked over my shoulder and said, "Kunta's here."

This was the nickname Ascot had given him before even meeting him, claiming Dele was "too African" for me. Ascot suggested I needed a "cornfed brotha named Tyrone," not an African from Africa with a pseudo-British accent. "How do you know?" I asked. "You'll see," he said.

Kunta walked up to the bar wearing a linen blazer with wide, bright red and white vertical stripes all over it, contrasting starkly against his dark black skin, making him look like a giant African candy cane.

Later, after Ascot left, Kunta said, "You haven't said you like my jacket."

"Oh, haven't I?" I smiled.

A little later, an older man who was next to us at the bar complimented Kunta on his jacket and he said, "See??" As if I were the only human being on the planet who couldn't recognize his impeccable taste in gaudy jackets.

My Attire: Even though he complimented my ass in jeans, Dele only ever wanted me to wear short skirts or dresses around him. He accused me of looking like I was going to work one night instead of out to dinner, despite my shirred tight-fitting black dress and high-heeled ankle boots, which I thought were kind of hot. He insisted I change into a shorter skirt before we left my apartment.

"Seriously?" I asked. "You really want me to change?"

"Short skirt!" he yelled from the living room.

"But it's 35 degrees outside and I'm 45 years old!"

"Short skirt!"

Baby mama: Dele suggested that I meet his daughter one weekend (too early, in my opinion) and I told him that if we were to do that, he might want to first mention it to his baby mama, because I think that's the right thing to do—out of respect for her. I know how uncomfortable I felt when my ex-husband introduced our daughter to a woman he was dating without letting me know first, and I found out from Imogen herself.

"Respect???" he screamed. "Fuck that bitch. I don't have one iota of respect for her. She doesn't deserve my respect."

This seemed like an overly and alarmingly negative reaction to my suggestion, steeped in bitterness and anger toward the mother of his child—who really didn't seem that bad from his earlier description of her.

Anal Sex: Note previous discussion with C-Lo about cleaning the chocolate chimney—and I don't mean sweet, delicious skin-chocolate, either. Dele's constant harping about how much he wanted anal was accomplishing the opposite of his intention. He barked the request like an order, which I found particularly unsexy. For the record, it never happened.

Conversing: He accused me of interrupting him constantly, but I thought that was called having a conversation. You know, like when you say something in response to someone when they pause after they say something?

Cursing: Apparently, he had never before met a woman with such a foul mouth. To this, I said, "Well, fuck that shit." He didn't even snicker. This was ironic, considering the dirty cock talk he liked to have in bed.

Red Wine: I suppose I lack taste because I don't drink red wine. I actually very much enjoy red wine but some bullshit about sulfites or some shit gives me headaches. So I avoid it and drink white, which I also thoroughly enjoy. Why is this a problem?

Jesus: He wanted to know what *exactly* I would do if I learned that *in fact* Jesus Christ was indeed our savior. No, really, he asked me that. And he wanted an answer.

Kabbalah: I invited him to come to an introductory Kabbalah lecture with me, just to hear what it's all about. After all, some of its tenets had helped get me through a very difficult period in life. I had also learned quite a bit about Judaism, as well as the similarities among many religions such as Catholicism, Islam, and Buddhism. I thought he might find this interesting since he was quite religious and well-educated.

His answer was a flat out "No." Not even a polite "Maybe," or "I'll think about it," or "Thank you, but that doesn't really interest me," or "No, thank you." Just flat out "No." And then, after a pause, "Why do you waste your time on that?"

Match.com: Turns out that he HAD seen that I liked his photo on Match.com the first time, but hadn't been all that interested because my profile seemed "silly" and there weren't enough photos displaying my true beauty (five isn't enough?). According to his logic, I must have had something to hide, since, unlike him, I didn't share every photo ever taken of me in the last three years. But—lucky for me—he decided to give me a shot when I reached out a second time.

It became clear that Dele had been on his best behavior early on, but as he got more comfortable with me—as early as Date 3—he began to criticize me openly. His way of pointing out things that he didn't like or agree with was almost accusatory, as if everything were a matter of right and wrong and I was definitely wrong. Instead of defending my position, I just felt insecure. Is it any surprise that I'd lost some confidence along my path thus far and started to second-guess myself?

I read an inspirational quote on Instagram once that stuck with me: "Never write about a place until you're away from it, because it gives you perspective." (It's from Ernest Hemingway, for the record, and it took me about two hours to find it again and attribute it to the proper person, so can I get a high-five right now?).

Now that the Kunta experience is behind me, I can look back and see clearly that I allowed my insecurity to cloud my logic. I am glad that I took notes at the time on the things that he criticized me for, because sharing them now makes me realize that I was selling myself short. Plus it's all kinda funny at this point.

Email to Chloe:
"I think Kunta the Nigerian has some real issues, or he's just an asshole."

Dele and I had gone out for a drink and a bite and we got into this ridiculous spat. He called Facebook users "idiots," dismissed social networking, and made fun of me for Instagramming, before admitting he didn't know what Instagram was. I tried to defend and explain it, citing that it was actually part of my job as a marketer of pop culture to understand social networking and therefore participate. Our voices were actually raised in heated debate about it. But it was a lost cause; there was no telling this guy anything.

We got back to my apartment and after getting comfortable in bed, we sort of laughed it off, but inside, I was really kind of freaked out at how judgmental and insulting his whole aggressive tirade was. He told me how much he enjoyed me and loved how passionate I was (passion = arguing), and how he wished we'd met ten years earlier so we could have had a beautiful mixed-race baby together. Then he started complaining about how we hadn't seen each other in a week, which wasn't acceptable. So I explained (again) that I travel often for work (I just had spent a week in Seattle), and I prioritize time with my daughter (duh) when I return. I reminded him that since each of us had kids, finding free time could be difficult sometimes. He insisted I commit to twice a week, minimum. I said I would try. He said I would have to do more than try. I said all I could promise was that I'd do my best.

> **Kunta: What if your best isn't good enough?**
> **Me: Then I'm sorry.**
> **Kunta: You're sorry for what? I'll ask again, what**
> **if your best isn't good enough?**
> **Me: All I can do is my best. What more can I do?**
> **If my best is not good enough for you, then**
> **I am sorry.**

Kunta: (silence)
Me: Wow, you didn't get *anything* you came for
      tonight, did you?

This was a joke. As in, "You drove all the way from New Jersey to see me tonight and you accomplished nothing." I had my period, so there would be no sex. Of course he had brought up anal sex, which we already know was not happening. We had previously discussed going on a vacation together. When he brought it up on this night, he said his dream vacation for us was to take a private car on an Amtrak train across the country. Please. Also, I had no red wine at my apartment and he didn't want any *white wine* (read with condescending tone). So, he'd achieved zero of his agenda items, Amtrak, red wine, and anal sex.

Kunta: (not acknowledging above joke) You're
      ***sorry*? Like, you're sorry, *that's IT for us*?**
Me: (shrugging, nodding yes, shaking my head
      no, I don't know, I guess...)
Kunta: That's it. I'm out of here.

He got up and started getting dressed. He was prone to teasing me and pulling practical jokes, which is a whole other annoying trait I neglected to mention earlier. I read once that practical jokes are a form of abuse, like tickling. You think it's all in fun but it's really a form of control and abuse. It's mean. So, I thought he was pulling one of his odd, unfunny practical jokes and I didn't react. I just stayed put.

Kunta: I'm leaving.
Me: OK...(still thinking he's kidding)...those are
my jeans, don't put those on.
Kunta: Right. OK, I'm out.
Me: OK, then. (Sarcastically) Buh-bye.

I didn't think he was actually leaving. I still thought this was a trick and he intended to upset me for his own amusement, then revel in the hilarity of my reaction to the news that he was kidding. But this time, I thought, "I'll beat this prick at his own game by not reacting." I was kicking back in my bed, checking my phone, when he slinked off into the foyer. I heard him putting his shoes on and then I heard the front door open and close.

I still thought he was faking it. I thought he opened and closed the door for effect and was still standing inside, possibly stifling an evil laugh. I lay in bed listening to the silence, afraid to move. Was he going to jump out of the shadows and scare the shit out of me? Was he just lurking by the front door after pretending to go through it? It was so quiet. Should I get up? Then, I heard a car engine start outside. After a few minutes of holding my breath and listening quietly to see if he was still here, I got up to look out the window. His car was gone!

Holy Fuck. What a dramatic exit! He actually left?! Did he expect me to beg him to return? Well, I didn't! What a relief to a very uncomfortable evening. I knew this relationship, after three months, was doomed. But was I up for the challenge of ending it? I was out of practice being the breaker-uppper, having recently only been the breaker-uppee. So who would be the first to bring up the "need to talk"? Where would it take place? How would it go down? But *this*! *This* was a graceful, easy exit served up on a convenient platter. It couldn't possibly have been this easy to close the Kunta chapter. I drew window blinds closed, hoping this was actually as easy a getaway as it seemed, and that this was a problem that just solved itself.

CHAPTER 7
UNABOMBER

Around 4:00 p.m. the next day, I received a Unabomber Manifesto-style email from Kunta about how I'm clearly not the right woman for him. It included a long laundry list of my faults and the situations where I didn't act or react the "right" way. Because of this, according to him, I'm obviously not ready for a real relationship as I'm not willing to compromise. Of course, I don't believe any of this is true. Although, it IS possible after spending five years compromising on so many levels with MD, I did want some things "my way or no way," as Kunta put it. There could be a grain of truth there. But I do believe there are things worth compromising for and anal sex and Amtrak are not on that list.

Disregarding all of his accusations, assumptions, and insults, I responded with a succinct email saying, funny, I'd thought the same thing about him: "It's your way, or no way. But thanks for some nice times nonetheless, and I wish you all the best." Then, I deleted all the emails and deleted him from my contacts.

About eight minutes later, I got a text from a 201 number, saying, "Is this really what you want? Or do you want to repair things?" It would have been hilarious if I'd responded, "Sorry, who is this??" But I knew it would only be hilarious to me and maybe to whomever I told the story to later. It was Memorial Day weekend so I responded by saying that we should reconsider over the long weekend and touch base next week.

For some reason, maybe because I liked the sex or maybe because I wanted a more mature closure—or maybe I just wanted to prove to him that I actually was a nice person—I agreed to meet him for a drink. And just to prove my willingness to compromise, I trekked all the way to the Upper West Side in the pouring rain, to a place of his choosing.

After an awkward greeting and some small talk, he asked me why I'm so "dramatic" and "crazy." He then confessed he was dealing with his "abandonment issues" in therapy and dropped this bomb about how his father abandoned him and his family, leaving his poor mother to raise three kids. He said he always fears abandonment, so his tactic is to be the abandoner and not the abandonee in relationships at the first sign of trouble.

MD had one of those abandoning fathers, too; his was an alcoholic. Why do I always pick guys who have daddy issues?

I agreed to give us another shot.

Email from Chloe:

WHY, bitch?? WHY? Why are you going out with the African Candy Cane again? You had such an easy exit. Now it's gonna get messy all over again. Just walk away, already. You don't have to make him like you before you decide

you never want to see him again. I know you want a steady dick in your life, but don't be desperate and settle on this asshole who only made you miserable. No dick is worth it if you feel less than the superwoman that you are. He is heinous. Run away!

Bitch knows me so well. I think I had to prove something, like Chloe said. I just wanted to prove that I DID try to make it work so that when (not if, but when) we decided to stop seeing each other, Kunta would know that I gave it my best shot and tried not to insist on "my way or no way." I'd never had the chance to execute a mutual break-up with Ethan (nor with my ex-husband for that matter), so somehow this felt like it would be a win for me.

Kunta and I made a plan for me to drive out to his apartment made entirely of drywall, in a vibe-free, sterile, still unfinished suburb of New Jersey, near the Meadowlands, on a Tuesday night after my Kabbalah class.

Let's take a moment to note all the compromises in this scenario.

First, I, a city dweller, cannot easily jump in my car and go. It requires calling the garage twenty-four hours ahead to arrange to pick up the car at an exact time or be scolded by the Latino parking attendant for being late and then tipping $2. (Maybe that sounds a little selfish but other New Yorkers will feel me on this.) My Kabbalah class starts at 7:00 p.m. and runs until about 8:15. After a long day's work, and seventy-five minutes of heavy and deep spiritual study, I generally like to take a leisurely walk home while peacefully contemplating the night's lecture. But in this case, I had to rush off as if my class were just another appointment, possibly to prove a point to Kunta that yes, I do know how to compromise and prioritize a relationship. I had to grab some food, get to the garage, then drive twenty-five minutes, putting me at his place around 9:00 p.m. When you really want to see someone, these are minor inconveniences. But I didn't, so they weren't. The plan was that I would stay over at his place and we'd drive back into the city together in my car on Wednesday morning (sitting in rush hour traffic, note further compromise).

I arrived just after 9:00 p.m. There was no food there, so luckily I had picked up a salad, which I ate. He opened some disgusting, sweet white wine (a nice attempt, I guess, at pouring me what I wanted). We watched the NBA Finals. We fucked on the couch while watching the game; then he went down on me while I watched Lebron James and Dwayne Wade sweat all over the court, which was the actual turn-on. It felt empty and odd, and not unlike pleasuring myself while watching an NBA game alone on my couch. We then retired to opposite sides of his bed. He was in boxers, as usual, and the socks that he always wore during sex. He read a book on his iPad while I tried to fall asleep, as if we were some kind of comfortable married couple. I listened to him fart in his sleep. He got up ridiculously early to get ready for work and woke me up, saying, "Come on, get up, chop chop! We have to leave in five minutes."

Five minutes??? I was pissed that he didn't give me more warning but in a way, it was fine to have only five minutes to race the fuck outta there. I got my shit together as quickly as possible, making an intentional effort to bring all my belongings with me.

"Come on! Every minute counts!" he coached from the sidelines.

On the way to the city he:

1. Didn't let me take a shortcut I know like the back of my hand because I've been traveling it for the last twenty-three years, for fear I would "get lost."
2. Criticized my downshifting (it's a manual transmission), accusing me of just liking "to feel that shifter in your hand."
3. When not challenging my driving or navigation abilities, read a book on his iPad, ignoring me. (It was the same book from the previous night—must have been a real page-turner.)
4. Insisted that I drop him off in front of his office on Wall Street, right in the heart of heavy downtown traffic.

I suggested dropping him off about five blocks away, to avoid lower Broadway, and he relented—so at least I sort of won that little battle. We said a fast, awkward goodbye as he jumped out curbside at a red light. I held my breath until the light changed, then exhaled a huge sigh of relief as I drove away and cranked up my car radio. I knew without a doubt that I would never see him again.

Email to Chloe:

Yah bish, you were right. I was trying to prove something with that one! I wanted him to know that all his accusations about me were wrong— that it wasn't just my way or no way. He had opened up a little bit by telling me about his abandonment issues, so I thought it might be different this time around. He seemed like he wanted a relationship as much as I did. So, I was trying to prove to him that I am nice and that he played a big a part when the road got bumpy. If he recognized that, and acted accordingly, maybe there was hope for us. But I didn't prove anything by going out to New Jersey except that he is in fact a giant dick. When I first met him, he was like a different guy who won me over, clearly not the true Dele. Or Kunta. The African Candy Cane. He is a dick. That's all it proved.

• • •

Earlier in the day of my final Kunta date, I had been in meetings near Union Square. On my way home, I stopped by Ace Sports to see if they had a very specific hand wrap I had been looking for to put under my boxing gloves. The guy who helped me was very flirty. I bought nothing from him, but I did manage to get an invitation to have a drink, and I walked out with his phone number and first name, Zander.

While I'd been driving to Kunta's that night, Zander and I were texting to make arrangements for our date on

Sunday night. I had actually missed the exit off of Route 17 because I was distracted by Zander's texts. When I texted Kunta to tell him I would be another ten minutes because I missed the exit, he gave me shit for being "a dingbat" and not recognizing the exit or driving too fast or downshifting or whatever other faults I was exhibiting by missing the exit.

CHAPTER 8
WHAT IS A FUCK BUDDY?

A fuck buddy is someone you fuck who is a buddy.

No, wait. A fuck buddy is someone you're attracted to, you go on a date and have sex with on the first date, all the while knowing deep down that there isn't much more you'd like to do with him except have sex, so you agree to continue doing that.

No, wait. A fuck buddy is a guy you really like who likes you, too. You spend some time together; enjoy having sex; talk about all kinds of fun things you're going to do together such as going on beach weekends, to the movies, to LA, to Miami. Then, at some point, you realize none of it will ever happen. There is a sort of understanding that it's all talk. Yet, you keep this buddy around to fuck. Maybe you think there is hope that these things will eventually happen. Maybe you believe that he actually did break up with his girlfriend and might have more time for you soon. So, you still share these ideas, talk about current events, enjoy a meal and some wine, but deep down you know full well that nothing will ever come of it. And yet you still fuck.

As suspected, nothing else ever happens. He's your buddy. You fuck him. End of story.

Fuck Buddy Rules:

Rule #1: Do not develop feelings for your fuck buddy. Do not develop feelings for your fuck buddy. Do not develop feelings for your fuck buddy. Do not develop feelings for your fuck buddy. Do not develop feelings for your fuck buddy. Do not develop feelings for your fuck buddy. Do not develop feelings for your fuck buddy. Do not develop feelings for your fuck buddy. Do not develop feelings for your fuck buddy. Do not develop feelings for your fuck buddy. Do not develop feelings for your fuck buddy. Do not develop feelings for your fuck buddy. Do not develop feelings for your fuck buddy. Do not develop feelings for your fuck buddy. Do not develop feelings for your fuck buddy. Do not develop feelings for your fuck buddy.

Rule #2: When the fucking changes, run away immediately and don't look back.

What constitutes "change"? If the sex...
- becomes less frequent;
- ceases to make you feel dirty, sexy, and hot;
- ceases to be satisfying;
- feels obligatory.

Or, most important,
- if you fake an orgasm because you just want him to stop already.

Rule #3: If Rule #1 fails, run away immediately and don't look back.

Rule #4: Have no regrets.

CHAPTER 9
ACE SPORTS

Email from Chloe:
Don't fuck that sales guy from the sporting goods store tonight. You are not that desperate. Go fuck one of those hot trainers, as least they have semi-real careers.

I wish I had known there were fuck buddy rules prior to my experience with Zander the Salesman. But I have written them in the wake of this experience so that you may be armed and ready if you ever enter into your own Fuck Buddy relationship.

Scooping up a salesman in a sporting good store isn't exactly my idea of finding true love, but since I was clearly skating on this side of unhappiness with my relationship with Kunta, it seemed like the thing to do at the time. I wouldn't even call the Kunta experience a "relationship"; it was more like a "situation" or an "experience," or even a "time frame." This guy Zander seemed like a nice option for distraction, extraction, and a new adventure.

When I approached the rack of boxing gloves and hand-wraps, I peripherally saw him make a beeline to me. It was like that move the vampires on *True Blood* do where one minute they're across the room and a split second later they are breathing down your neck. At first, I wasn't sure if this was aggressive salesman behavior, like "Oh, look at the woman who appears to have money. Let me sell her something she doesn't need and will never use." Or, if he just was going in for the flirt kill.

"Hullo, can I help ya?" He had a very thick New York accent and wore a giant cross around his neck. He had a hip leather man-bracelet on, and his tight-fitting Ace Sports uniform shirt showed off a nice physique. Those sales guys all work off commission, so whether they help you choose a pair of socks or a full size canoe, they "sticker" the price tag so they get credit for the sale. Well, Zander must have been pretty confident about selling shit left and right because his forearm was covered in stickers for easy access. I asked what he knew about hand wraps for under my boxing gloves. I wasn't sure what I wanted, so he allowed me to try a few on. To do this, I had to remove a couple of rings and put them randomly on other fingers, which made it look like I had a wedding ring on—and when I noticed this, I immediately rearranged the rings again. Pointing to the stickers running up his forearm, I flirtily asked. "Are you for sale, too?"

"Yes, for the right price, I am," he said in his thick accent.

I liked him right away for picking up on my stupid opening line and flirting back. That, and the fact that he didn't try to sell me those wraps. He totally understood that they were uncomfortable and just shrugged and said,

"I don't think you want those."

We chatted about boxing and other forms of working out, and this was the catalyst for the segue into full-on flirtation.

"I'm Zander" (pronounced: zee-AHN-duh, his accent making a two-syllable word into three), he said, and asked me if I was married. He'd seen me moving my rings around and wasn't sure where the little gold one belonged.

"Nope, not married."

"Would you like to join me for a drink some time?"

"Yes, sure, I'd love to."

"What about tonight? I get off work at 7."

I said I couldn't do it that night, so he gave me his card and told me to let him know when would be good. I started to explain that I had a ten-year-old daughter and a tough work schedule and he interrupted me and said, "I'm not looking to marry you."

This might have been a red flag for some women, but not me. I just kept yammering "Oh, haha, yes I know that, but my point was that my schedule can be difficult, so if it seems like I am never available, it doesn't meant that I'm not interested, it's just my schedule." He didn't seem to care much at all about that, and I just left it that I would be in touch.

I felt embarrassed as I made my way out of the store. I suspected I was one of many victims of the Vampire Salesman. There was a follow-spot on me as I left the store and all of the other employees were knowingly nodding and pointing at me, "Look, that dumb woman who was just flirting with Zander. He got her number. Man he is good, isn't he?" And then, "Hey, lady, do you give your number to all retail salesmen who show you a little attention? Is it that easy?"

I texted Zander when I got home, to (a) test the number and (b) kick it over to him to follow up, which he did, and we made plans for a drink on Sunday. The good news was that he didn't tell me to choose a place. The bad news was that he suggested we meet at the Blarney Stone, which as you may gather, is an Irish beer-drinking sports bar, probably with cedar chips on the floor. This is not my kind of establishment. It's a tough position to be in. A guy asks you out but suggests something other than the classy wine bar that you and your girlfriends so enjoy. Guys seem to think that just because you say you like sports (which I generally do), that it would be swell to meet at a place with twelve-page beer list, happy-hour prices, and multiple big-screen TVs.

I managed to talk him out of the Pig Whistle, or whatever it was, and we ended up at the very staid restaurant bar on the corner of my street. When I walked in, he was already sitting at the corner of the bar, beer in hand, chatting with the senior citizens enjoying their happy hour chardonnays. He welcomed me with a big smile and we proceeded to have a great time chatting and getting to know each other. We covered all of the typical first-date stuff: He was half Italian, half Spanish. His mother had passed, his father was a successful Spanish musician and quite the ladies man at age eighty-four. He lived on the Upper East Side in a tiny rent-stabilized apartment (*read: shithole*) that his family had been in for forty-plus years. He aspired to be a screenplay writer but was currently the top seller at Ace Sports, where he'd been employed for two years. He'd had a girlfriend for the last ten years but they recently separated because, while they loved each other, they were not "in love" anymore and she wanted to get married. He had a brother who was into the PX90 home workout and he wished he worked out more so that he could be more like me.

After more drinks, the food menu came. He ordered a burger from the bartender *"sin cebolla porque voy a besar la,"* which means, "with no onion because I'm going to be kissing her later." He asked me if I understood what he said. I admitted I understood the word *besar* so I figured it out. I told him that he was being awfully presumptuous, but I was barely able to finish my sentence before he started kissing me.

If there's one thing I enjoy, it's a good kisser. I was well aware that the top salesman at Ace Sports was not going to be my future husband, but I was also aware that he was going to be my future lover. The future came quickly: We ended up in my bed that very night.

Zander was very talented with his tongue and fingers. When I complimented him on his speedy delivery of my orgasm, he explained that because he himself had a hard time climaxing, he'd found ways to pleasure a woman without banging her to death while he tried to reach orgasm. The reason he had trouble coming, he said, is that he watched too much porn and jerked off all day. This is an interesting confession, coming from someone who has had a regular girlfriend for ten years. Perhaps he was bored of fucking her so he resorted to porn, but judging by his flirtatious manner and charm, I don't know why he couldn't just cheat on her. Come to think of it, I'm sure he did that as well.

"Best first date ever," I lied.

"We can be fuck buddies!" he exuberantly declared.

We had already discussed our mutual love of beaches, road trips, movies, and museums, so I was happy to know that I might have a summer-time companion to do fun stuff with, who would also fuck me regularly and all without any ties. At the time, I thought Zander the Vampire Salesman could be a perfect arrangement for companionship while I continued the hunt for permanent, trusty, and loyal dick.

• • •

We saw each other regularly for a few months. "Seeing each other regularly" entailed him coming over after his Ace Sports shift around 6:00 p.m., where we ate a quick, cheap bite of food and drank a bottle of cheap wine at my apartment while we talked or watched a movie, then ended up in bed. Sometimes he would sleep over. We got comfortable quickly and he kept a toothbrush in my bathroom. MD had never kept a goddamn toothbrush in my bathroom and I'd dated him for five years. Zander and I peed with the bathroom door open so that we could continue whatever conversation we happened to be having. But there was never a beach, road trip, or museum, and all movies were watched from the comfort of my couch.

One time, we took a bath with candles and bubbles. It felt sort of romantic for a second, as we softly kissed in the relaxing warmth, and he asked me "*¿Qué quieres?*

¿Quieres amor?" I pretended like I didn't understand because I was afraid to answer the question. Yes, I did *quiere amor*, but probably not with him. And if he was hinting that he *quiere'd amor* with me, then maybe I would consider stepping this up a notch; we'd have to be more than just being fuck buddies. We'd have to start getting out of the house and actually doing things. Then he grabbed the skin folds on his stomach and started making fart sounds while he moved his fat rolls open and closed like a mouth.

After only a short time seeing each other, we had done more fucking and coming and sleeping together in my bed than I had done with MD in five years. The comparison was not lost on me, though, the bar was set so low that it would not have been difficult for any man off the street to beat MD's record: Two orgasms and one or two nights at my apartment in five years. Those are some low-ass standards. At the same time, I was aware that I needed more than fucking and coming and a fuck-buddy relationship has an expiration date, which was nearing.

CHAPTER 10

FLIGHT TO NASHVILLE

Email to Chloe:

Yesterday I flirted with the Hot Flight Attendant, HFA, on my way to Nashville. He slipped me his # so I texted him at 500 feet. We texted back and forth all day about meeting up for a drink. So when my meetings were over at 11 pm, he came to my hotel and I fucked him.

Earlier that morning before the flight, I woke up with the Vampire Salesman in my bed. So, I pretty much had sex with two guys in one day. What is wrong with me?

Chloe asked for more details but it all happened so fast that there really weren't many to tell. Here they are, for those of you who might be interested.

I was flying to Nashville to attend meetings. My flight was delayed by about two hours. As happens often on flights from LaGuardia to Nashville, I saw a music business colleague at the gate, John. We commiserated about the delay, caught up on work topics, and had a pleasant visit.

When we finally boarded the flight, John and I sat near each other but not together. The hot, black flight attendant caught my eye immediately. As he put something in the overhead bin, I spied those muscles and thought, well this might just make up for the two-hour delay. But based on his neat-and-tidy style, trendy bracelets—and the fact that he was a flight attendant, hello—I suspected he was gay. But something about his demeanor suggested otherwise. As I considered this, an uppity-sounding British voice spoke through the PA, saying it was her pleasure to serve us, along with Ray.

Hmmm. Hello, Ray.

About an hour into the flight, Ray aka HFA (Hot Flight Attendant) admired my bracelet as I reached out to deposit a pile of magazines and papers into his trash bag. So, of course I admired his, too. We chatted about bracelets and our favorite cheap accessory stores (gay?). He eventually had to get back to his job collecting trash so I said, "You know where to find me." I let out one of those loud, uneasy guffaws that happen when you laugh awkwardly at your own joke.

Because of the two-hour delay, my Nashville plans had to be adjusted. I would have to go straight to a lunch meeting from the airport instead of checking in to the hotel first. As you can imagine if you were paying attention to above email to Chloe, I felt gross from the previous night's shenanigans and needed a refresher-upper. So I decided to change my clothes and apply some makeup while on the plane. I headed back to the tiny bathroom with my little black dress and makeup kit. I found HFA kicking back in the aisle seat directly across from the bathroom door, listening to music or doing something on his phone. I asked him if it was OK if I used the bathroom to change my clothes quickly, even though the seatbelt sign was on. He encouraged me to and said to take my time.

I only half closed the little folding door because I figured I would just quickly lift one dress over my head, throw the other dress on in mere seconds, and then do my makeup with the door half ajar so that I could (a) make myself available to chat with HFA, (b) make a beeline out of the bathroom if need be, since the seatbelt sign was illuminated, and (c) not hog the bathroom and prevent someone else from actually using it.

I'd barely wiggled out of one sleeve when someone banged loudly on the door. The uppity British voice yelled at me to return to my seat.

"Be right out!" I yelled, as I scrambled to get undressed and redressed. I flung the door open and shot a WTF look at HFA, who shrugged, slid over to the window seat, and patted the aisle seat cushion for me to sit next to him.

He explained that the Brit was a bit uppity (as I'd suspected). Actually, the words he used were, "She ain't cool." I got the impression that HFA had a reputation for being overly friendly with passengers and his co-flight attendant wasn't having it. Her banging on the door wasn't so much directed at me, but more toward HFA, with his lackadaisical approach to safety and for his prioritizing flirting over FAA regulations and air protocol.

Once the seatbelt sign was off, I popped back into the bathroom to quickly apply blush and some eyeliner and mascara. I explained my situation to HFA, who had kindly and sweetly said, "You don't need all that." So now, with my cute dress on and feeling a little more attractive, I sat back down with HFA to continue what I'd started. When work-guy John came back to use the bathroom and found me sitting in a seat that clearly wasn't mine chatting away with the flight attendant, he gave me an awkward, "Oh, hello…?" I just shrugged and smiled.

It was a short flight so there wasn't a whole lot of flight attending to do; no meals to serve, just one round of drinks and the cleanup. So HFA and I were able to spend some quality time getting to know each other.

• • •

HFA wasn't at the lowest level of strangers I have met with one clear objective, but he was no rocket scientist either. He was good for a couple laughs, some stories, and a very handsome smile. We joked about how there's nothing for him to do when he's stuck at airport hotels and he generally doesn't hang around with the other crewmembers. I tried to encourage him to go into the city of Nashville, have a look around, that sort of thing, but that didn't really seem to interest him. He was more concerned with working out at the hotel gym (points!) and drinking the miniature liquor bottles he regularly stole from flights.

Eventually, HFA did need to do his job so I returned to Seat 8A, making the same stupid joke about how he would know where to find me and expecting a laugh this time. I still didn't get one. The plane was making its initial descent and HFA was trash collecting again. I panicked. Do I slip him my number? Do I just de-plane with no follow through? Do I ring my call button?

On his final pass through the cabin, HFA handed me a folded-up slip of paper towel with his name (Ray, not HFA) and number scrawled on it and suavely said, "Let me know..." I smiled and said "OK, great," or something like that. I texted him before the plane even touched down.

We continued to text throughout the day and he made it abundantly clear he wanted to get laid...I mean, *see me*. I let him know that my dinner meeting would probably go until late, and he told me he had to be on the shuttle van to the airport at 5:00 a.m. When I asked him how late was too late to come to my hotel for a drink, he said, "5:00 a.m., because that's when I have to leave for the airport, lol. I really want to c u." I assumed at this point, despite the bracelets, that he was not gay.

It was 11:30 p.m. when HFA arrived at the hotel. When I greeted him in the lobby with my heels on, I noticed he was way shorter than he appeared on the plane and also Puerto Rican, not black. Also, he was more *cute* than *hot*, so CFA, I guess.

We were in the heart of Nashville, supposedly a hotbed of activity, but everything was closed in the hotel. No bar, no restaurant, no sports bar, nothing. I asked one of the employees where we could have a drink. Was there a wine bar nearby? We're in downtown Nashville, after all, where's all the action?

Apparently, wine bars in this city are a foreign concept and all the action is on Broadway. Bar after bar after bar was indeed open, but each of them had loud country music cover bands performing. This was the total opposite of what I had in mind for my drink with the flight attendant. Why was there no hotel bar in my own respectable Hilton? I mean, isn't that where lonely travelers and flight attendants regularly find each other?

Eventually, we followed the directions of the bellboy, who said there was *one* bar he knew of that didn't have live music. It turned out to be a smoky dive with a jukebox so loud, there might as well have been a band. At first it was fine. HFA talked a lot without asking me much about myself. I listened politely to lots of mundane details about his buddies, their annual trip to the "swinger's hotel" in Cancun, his kid, his baby mama, and his monthly flight route and the art of stealing miniatures from the service carts.

Back in my hotel lobby, we started what I thought was going to be a make-out session in front of the late-night hotel staff. But then, the suggestion of going up to my room came with the promise of "you'll be more comfortable," with which I could not argue. Once he stopped talking and started kissing me, the attraction, that had eluded me during all that yammering, came back. He was a good kisser, indeed. After a brief kissing frenzy on the couch, the disrobing began. Evidently, I was indeed more comfortable, and the application of the condom followed shortly thereafter.

HFA was a soft and gentle kisser and a very nice lover. He explored me with his tongue and fingers, then we fucked in a few different positions (definitely not gay). It was nice, comfortable, easy, and safe. So why did I feel so low and disgusting when he left?

• • •

The next morning, I was semi-mortified. After taking a very rigorous shower and washing my pussy like seven times, I decided to test the waters to see if that was truly a one-night stand with a complete stranger, old-school style, or if there might be repeat performances in the future. Because that's just what I needed—another Fuck Buddy.

I texted HFA something along the lines of, "Hope you didn't miss your flight. Thanks for a fun night." I got what may or may not have been an obligatory, "lol that was fun. I'll let u know when I'm back in NYC" response.

The fact that I got an immediate text back made me feel only slightly less disgusting. I headed down to the hotel lobby after only four hours of strange and uncomfortably hot hotel sleep, still feeling like an exceptionally ho-ish dirty slut. None of my business colleagues were there yet, so I sat down in the lobby with a coffee to wait for them and the car to the airport. As I read through my emails, I was greeted with the news that the first release on my brand-new record label was #1 on the *Billboard* Top New Artist Album Chart. Our first release scored a #1! That's way hotter than a black and/or Puerto Rican stranger on a plane. It's nice to keep things in perspective sometimes.

CHAPTER 11

NASHVILLE, PART *DOS*

Surprisingly, HFA and I stayed in touch. Staying in touch in this case meant a few "how r u"-style texts along with a myriad of dick pics.

He asked for photos in return, opening the door for some creative sexting. I really wasn't sure how to go about taking dirty selfies, but I was game to try. The first thing that occurred to me was that I shouldn't include my face, lest said image end up on the Internet somewhere.

I remembered a photo Ascot had shown me from some girl he was sexting with. It was her naked body in a very classy, sexy, red-carpet-style leg-forward pose. It made her body and especially her legs look amazing. The photo was taken in a full-length mirror with her head cut off. I decided to try to replicate this photo, and got undressed. The lighting in my bedroom was harsh no matter how much I adjusted it. My skin looked pale, my nipples looked like two giant melted Hershey Kisses, and my neck skin looked old. This wasn't as easy as I'd thought, but I was determined to capture something sexy and classy that showed at least a little of the body I work so hard to maintain. With a little experimentation, moving to the bathroom where the lighting was warmer and there was a dimmer, I shot a winning photo. It showed my six-pack abs, my sexy legs, my Brazilian no-hair crotch area, and best of all, no head.

The photo went over big-time. In fact, it was so well received that I archived it in a secret hiding place on my phone and used it again and again in the future. However this one glamour shot wasn't enough for HFA. He didn't want classy, arty, well-lit nude photos, he wanted straight up pussy shots. "Lemme see more," he texted.

I wasn't comfortable with this concept yet, so I said OK but never delivered. He sent me a few more dick pics over the next few weeks, one of which he sent TWICE and I thought maybe he was sending dick pics all over the place and had forgotten which ones he sent to which girl in which city. So I told him that I didn't want any pre-owned dick pics and if he was going to keep sending them, he had to show me a photo of his dick with today's paper.

For the record, I also received G-rated photos of him...one in a car, another with his kid, and one dancing with friends at a club (sorta gay?). He sent a big close-up smiley photo of himself on the plane and a super-goofy one where he was wearing a pair of silly bright neon green sunglasses shaped like stars. With all of the sweet photos mixed in with the dick pics and videos, I wasn't sure exactly what we were doing. One day, it was his handsome smiling face with his gorgeous kid in the car seat behind him, and the next day it was an iPhone video of him jerking himself off in a Best Western with ESPN on in the background. It's a little confusing for a girl.

We eventually made a plan to meet in New York when he had some time off after a morning flight. I felt a little weird about him coming over, so I gave him the cross streets of my apartment without actually giving him my address. I am not sure what good I thought this would do, knowing eventually he would end up in my bed. I guess I didn't want to text my address in case he, or someone close to him with access to his phone, decided to stalk me.

I met him downstairs sort of on the side of my apartment entrance. He looked hot—just as handsome, if not more so, as I remembered and very fit. I wore flats intentionally to adjust for height. We hugged and kissed and it was actually very nice to see him. In fact, it almost felt like something real. There was a definite attraction, for sure, and I was feeling a little excited about his exotic-ness: A flight attendant (I could fly for free), Puerto Rican (a place to visit), the ultimate sexy Latin lover (yum). After a little debate about "what do you want to do…" knowing full well what was inevitable, we went to a diner for breakfast. We had mimosas, then stopped by the liquor store and the grocery store to get mimosa supplies to continue the party.

He thought it was weird that we had to go to two stores. "Just get the champagne here," he said at the grocery store. I tried to explain that in New York City, they don't sell alcohol in the grocery store, nor do they sell groceries in the alcohol store. He was having a hard time wrapping his head around this because in Fort Lauderdale, where he lives, the strip mall grocery store is one-stop shopping. He was also a little complain-y about having to walk an extra block and back. Also, I paid for both items.

We got back to my apartment where he made himself at home immediately. He kicked off his shoes, headed straight to the kitchen, and as if he already knew where the champagne glasses were kept, poured two perfect orange-to-champagne-ratio mimosas. We played house, we played couple (or at least I did, in the privacy of my mind), and we stole kisses in between pouring. We sat down on the couch, close, touching, rubbing, feeling. We chatted...well actually, much like our first date in Nashville, he chatted. I learned all about his brother who works at the Plaza Hotel as a doorman and makes big tips, his sister who works at the Cartier store selling fancy watches, his mother who just wants the best for all her kids but still lives in the projects in the Bronx. He also told me flight attendant stories, most of which were not very exciting, with the exception of one.

Email to Chloe:
   HFA, the hot flight attendant was here earlier today, we had mimosas.
   Hot sex.
   Dumb as fuck.
   But very manly, as he told me stories of taking control of an inept flight crew in a scary flight situation.
   Hot sex again.

Hot sex. I mean REALLY good sex. Fucking like I have not had in many years. Great fucking. I had a vaginal orgasm, that kind of great fucking. That kind of thing does not come along every day. It's special, unique, and very fucking rare.

Then I had to transform back into my responsible self, the self who doesn't day-drink and fuck strangers in the middle of a workday. I had a conference call at 3:00 p.m. so I had to kick him out. As we were getting dressed, he took a phone call in Spanish and yelled really loud at whomever was on the phone, which was odd. I pretended not to notice. We said a sweet goodbye, but there was no mention of seeing each other again or anything of the sort. I was surprised to be a little disappointed about that.

• • •

And the dick pics ensued. Hall-of-Fame dick pics. Also videos. This time he insisted that I reciprocate, and considering he'd made me come like I haven't come in years, I thought it was the least I could do. I experimented with angles, lighting, and positioning until I'd snapped enough photos of various body parts to keep in my secret photo-hiding place to dole out upon future requests. We exchanged these sorts of photos for the next few weeks.

A couple weeks later, I picked HFA up at the airport— which, according to Ascot, is "a boo's job." I knew I was no boo, but the car was out of the garage anyway. Also, the dude would have taken like an hour and half to get to my apartment because he is frugal (*read: cheap*) and would have taken the subway from the airport. So it was a selfish move to get the party started earlier. When he got in the car, he surprised me by kissing me like a boo—a long, intense, soft, and sweet kiss. Again, this made me question for a split second what exactly we were doing here.

We talked a lot as we drove, made jokes, and the conversation flowed a little better than it had before. He told me he had been a dancer in Florida, hence the photo of him and his friends in the club dancing (still not gay). After we parked the car, we went to the wine store and back to my place. He made comments about not knowing what I would want to do so he hadn't made any specific plans or been sure of what clothes to bring. I said it was fine to just chill. He suggested movies, the club, dancing, dinner, a long walk. I said let's just go to my apartment for now, but I am open to any of those things with some advance planning. He said, "Good to know for the future." I was still confused about what we were doing.

Talk a little, drink wine, fuck all night. And I mean all night. ALL. FUCKING. NIGHT. I think he drank two bottles of wine himself and started acting quite drunk. At one point we took a break from fucking and when he went to the kitchen to get water he tripped over some furniture and made a major racket. I was afraid the downstairs neighbors would come banging on the door to see if I was OK.

Then he couldn't come. It took for fucking ever and I was deliriously exhausted. At one point he said, "I want to feel you inside me." Isn't that my line? Earlier I had asked him if he was staying the night and he answered, "I don't care!" What kind of an answer is that? I wasn't sure if it was an English-isn't-my-first-language thing or a drunk thing or just the straight-up truth. The whole night ended up kind of weird and he did sleep over. Or more like napped over.

After getting like three hours of sleep and being totally hung over, I had to go to the gym to meet my current actual trainer (to work out, to be clear. The trainers I actually work out with are off limits). After the exhausting and odd night of fucking, HFA's inability to come for an eternity, his odd behavior and drunkenness, I sort of wanted him out of my apartment. The training appointment was a good excuse to get out the door. HFA walked me to the gym and I must say the goodbye was, again, very sweet. It didn't feel one-night-stand-like. It still felt like he might actually like me. But because I was still unsure of what I liked at this point, I said goodbye a block before the gym, hoping that the Original-Soul-Fucker-Who-Shall-Not-Be-Named or HDT or HCT didn't see me kissing a Puerto Rican flight attendant on the street corner.

• • •

That was the last time I saw HFA, but that was my doing. The dick pics and texts and "hey are you in NY" and "hey stranger" and "hey you" texts kept coming. I didn't stop responding at first—I guess I wanted to keep the door ajar—but I started to feel empty and low again. I didn't really need another fuck buddy, though he was a good replacement for the Vampire Salesman, who had disappeared by this point.

About six months later, HFA asked me if I had "done it" with anyone else since I last did it with him. I answered truthfully (yes), but I still don't know why he asked. Was I supposed to ask him the same thing? I definitely didn't want to know the answer so I left it alone.

HFA never suggested actually making a plan to see each other or taking a trip together, or me visiting Fort Lauderdale. The movies, dancing, and dinner ideas never came up again either. The texts were always just about whether or not I was in New York at the moment and could I not send my daughter to her dad's for the night so he could come over. I mean, I might have been a little more inclined to stay with the program if there were ever any mention of actually enjoying my company or wanting to see me. The smallest bit of flattery might have gone a long way. As it was, it started to feel like less like two people getting to know each other and more like a meaningless hookup that, although sexually satisfying, was ultimately unsatisfying.

Inevitably, the void-of-substance texts just became annoying. So I stopped responding. I'll still get one every blue moon that says "Hey u. U in ny?" I may or may not respond.

CHAPTER 12

DATE A BLACK GUY WITH A JOB DOT COM

OK enough already. I had proven to myself (and everyone else) that I could nail a younger man. I was a MILF, I was sexy, I was desirable. Check. I had had my fun and it was time to behave like a grownup. I had had plenty of orgasms since MD, so I was feeling like a real woman once again. It was time to focus my energy on something lasting. That's what I really wanted, wasn't it?

But, Jesus. How do you meet real men? Everyone seems to have such great success stories from Match.com, but I was so disgusted by the choices, the approaches, the lack of proper spelling and grammar. The profiles were so egomaniacal and demanding. If guys only knew how they sounded. Is there some kind of template with suggestions on how to describe yourself and what you're looking for? There must be, because all the profiles sounded the same to me. Here are some annoying phrases I came across over and over ad nauseam.

- I live life to the fullest.
- I am an easy-going guy.
- I am a simple man.

- I am a God-fearing man.
- No drama, please.
- I am looking for a woman who is comfortable in both a dress and in jeans.
- I enjoy all sports, especially football.
- My two kids are the center of my world.
- I want a woman who (fill in the blank). I want, I want, I want.

And the most insufferable dating profile *faux pas* of all:

- You should be... (fill in the blank).

Now, I know that it's just semantics, but don't tell me what I should be. I am who I am; you like it or you don't. I should be who I am. Being on the receiving end of this language feels insulting; it's presumptuous, as if a man is making demands on you before you even meet him.

I couldn't help but feel defensive when I read some of these profiles, like I wanted to reply:

Listen, motherfucker. You are NOT easy going at all. You are demanding, picky, closed-minded and stuck in your ways. You have just as much baggage as any woman, with your divorce and your kids and your mid-life-crisis penis car. Also, don't tell me you work out 4-5 times a week when I can see that gut. And if you love to travel so much, why are all your photos in the bathroom, in your foyer, in your car with the seatbelt on, and in your backyard? That's not living life to the fullest, as far as I can tell. And that one photo

on Machu Picchu (or Golden Gate Bridge or similar cliché landmark) doesn't count.

Furthermore, when you reach out to me in an email, say something more than 'how r u?' I will tell you now, I am fine, thanks, now say something of substance. Did you read my profile? Ask me something about it or compliment me. And don't just say "hello," either. Hello, yes, hello already. Boring. Then again, if I have to tell you all this, don't fucking bother.

All the messages from fat, balding, pasty, vanilla guys were depressing and demotivating. Where was all the delicious chocolate? Wasn't there someone like me? Attractive, in shape, slightly exotic, well-traveled, and young at heart? Why was everyone so seemingly desperate and pedestrian? I wished there were something like "Date a Hot Black Guy with a Job Dot Com."

So I Googled that. And somehow I stumbled upon a website for exactly that. Seriously, try it. Google "date a hot black guy" and see what happens.

This is not to say that I wouldn't ever date a hot guy (black or otherwise) without a job, for the record. As you probably know by now, up to this point I hadn't been quite so picky. But at this particular moment in my dating life, I'd had enough of the starving artist type. "Anyone With A Job Dot Com" sounded pretty good, too. This is also not to say that I am making some kind of statement about who has jobs and who doesn't. Lots of guys don't have jobs, I just wasn't interested in dating them. Anymore. I already did. In general, at a certain point in your life, you want the guy you date to be somewhat employed, no?

Anyway, upon my Google search, I discovered InterracialDating.com, and mama was home. I excitedly and speedily jammed out a profile, plunked my credit card down for the "three-month best value," and sat back and watched the winks and emails flood in.

I'm not even kidding. The skies had cleared, the sun was shining, and the angels were singing. I got something like three hundred views in twelve minutes. The vultures gathered and circled, ready to pounce on the pretty new white girl, and I had hit the dating website jackpot.

Look at all these potential blackguyswithjobs! I spent the next three days managing the sudden tidal wave of attention. My profile was viewed 653 times in three days and I am not exaggerating.

Here is a sampling of some of the more creative screen names:

Needubabe
HotSBM4U
UrNewBF
Living4Love
MrFixItGood4U
EpicManliness
KinkyLuv

And my personal favorite...
Freak11Plus (think about it).

• • •

It didn't stop. I created chaos in my search for love and sex and attention. Between the guys from the websites, the trainers at the gym, and the parade of guys who found their way into my bed, the noise was deafening. The constant barrage of texts from HDT, HCT, Sergeant GoMets, Officer Foot Fetish, HFA Ray, the Vampire Salesman, and Soul Fucker were overwhelming. And all of a sudden, HMN was back and Kunta emailed me.

I just wanted it all to stop.

I had met Hector, you see. He found me on DateABlack GuywithAJobDotCom. His screen name was simply Mr. HH (which, ironically, didn't stand for Hot Haitian or anything of the sort; it was his actual initials). His email just said, "You are gorgeous. What makes you happy?" That made an immediate impression on me, a seemingly more honest approach than such grammar and spelling atrocities as "how r u?" or "your funny" (to which I like to reply, "my funny what?") or "would like to get 2 no u." Hector's opener didn't consist of that many words but each one was spelled right, properly capitalized, and not abbreviated. This goes a long way with me.

I wasn't sure I was interested at first. He seemed handsome in a unique way but not really my type. I showed Chloe some of his photos and told her, "I am not into that cue-ball look, but if I saw that on the beach, I would definitely look twice." He'd included lots of location photos: beaches, cityscapes, forest areas, all suggesting he was an avid traveler like me. His profile stated that traveling was his biggest passion. There were no other people in the exotic photos, just him. One photo in particular, with a backdrop of Singapore, looked

Photoshopped and I suspected it was fake. Maybe they were *all* fake. What if this guy Photoshopped himself into all these different scenes to create the illusion he was a world traveler? There was no one else in them, after all. Imagine my shock when we first met and he told me that he ran the photo-retouching department at a major photography studio. He assured me he hadn't actually Photoshopped himself into any of the photos on his profile but he did like to use photo effects which sometimes create a fake look. Today, anyone can create those looks with the readily available iPhone and Instagram effects, but at the time, you had to have a specific app to do that, so I had no reason not to believe him.

We hit it off immediately. We were holding hands within the first ten minutes. After I admired his bracelet made of little black skulls, he said, "I'll get you one, so you have one, too." I didn't really want one for myself necessarily, I was admiring it on him, but how could I decline such a romantic offer?

We started dating regularly. Everything clicked. Everything was easy. Nothing seemed out of place, and finally, I felt excited about having a real relationship. We discovered so many things in common. This was an experience I'd not had for years…if ever: dating a man and discovering common interests, getting each other's jokes, exchanging life stories, sympathizing, understanding.

On our fourth date, before we'd even had sex (look at me being all patient!), we planned a trip to Vancouver. Hector said that it was one of his favorite cities and he wanted to take me because I had never been. That night we had sex in my apartment. Was it sex or did we make love? It had been so long since I had anything but a fuck buddy that I wasn't quite sure. But I enjoyed it thoroughly. I found him to be a good lover and I knew this could be something right and steady for me. I was, of course, trepidatious, but it felt so good to have a real man like me for me, and not just for my tight pussy and sweet ass.

Hector slept over but said he had to get up super early to go meet his friend on Long Island to ride motorcycles. We were up until something like 3:00 a.m., and he had to leave at 7:00 a.m. After all I've been through, I assume everything is always a lie. I like sex, and guys smell that on me. So whenever they can get laid, they do. My fear is always that there is some other woman lurking in the background. Anyone who has to go somewhere at 7:00 on a Sunday morning is definitely hiding something.

But Hector texted me a photo of himself and his friend on their motorcycles, as if he somehow knew I might need proof. He told me that his friend saw how exhausted he was and asked him why he didn't just cancel. I asked him the opposite: Why didn't you just tell me you had somewhere to be and call it a night earlier? He told me that he didn't want our night to end or cut our time short by going to sleep. Being with me and enjoying our first big night together was more important. But he also didn't want to cancel on his friend because they had made these plans a while ago and were both looking forward to it. I thought this said a lot about Hector's character.

CHAPTER 13
PITBULL

Before I found DateABlackGuyWithAJobDotCom, I had seen a fantastic-looking print ad in the United Airlines in-flight magazine called "Let's Do Lunch." The ad promised that upwardly mobile professionals like myself, who don't have time to meet people, might enjoy meeting for lunch instead of drinks or dinner, since they are so busy. And, if there is no love connection, well, it's easy to bail out: It's just lunch. It was not cheap to join, so any man involved in it must be upwardly mobile and have a savings account.

At some low and desperate moment over the summer, I had signed up for Let's Do Lunch. The fucked up thing about this dating service, though, is that *they* are in control, not *you*. They act as matchmakers, pairing you with someone *they* choose for you. You don't even see a goddamn photo or a profile ahead of time. You do, however, get a phone call from the service beforehand, describing your date in a way that is meant to paint an accurate picture. This prodigious person they've found is supposed to match with you in some way that I am still to this day unclear about.

On paper, I was a forty-five-year-old divorcee with one child who worked in "the arts." In real life, I was a boy-crazy cougar who behaved like an obsessive teenager, acted twenty years younger than her age, and only wanted guys ten to twenty years younger who looked like Morris Chestnut in his *Nurse Jackie* role.

The first guy they forced upon me was Freddy, described in my phone call as a fifty-year-old divorced professional with two kids. According to the phone lady, he was "dark" in complexion and "handsome" in her estimation. I told her emphatically about one hundred times that I don't date guys my own age, but she assured me that they'd conducted in-depth interviews and they knew just who to match with whom.

I met Freddy at a restaurant at 7:00 p.m., which I balked at because it was supposed to be "lunch," dammit. I was the first to arrive. The maître d' had apparently been hipped to the situation, because when I ordered a glass of Pinot Grigio, he said, "Takes the edge off the nerves, right?" Maybe I *was* a little nervous. I was also annoyed that I had to wait for more than fifteen minutes. While sipping my wine, I slyly scoped out the room each time there was movement or a new person entered my peripheral vision. When a short, balding, coke-bottle-glasses-wearing Indian gentleman wearing a pink shirt that nicely showcased his gut walked in and started talking and nodding furiously with the maître d', I wanted to spontaneously combust and/or disappear. I glanced at my watch quickly and figured I could make polite conversation for an hour or so, then exit gracefully. This would be my punishment for having joined such a site and for trusting their description of Freddy.

Somehow, Freddy wasn't so bad. He was friendly and sort of funny and a bit sarcastic. But he was a low talker so I found myself saying "What?" "Pardon?" "Excuse me?" a little too often for comfort. When he invited me to dinner, I thought, "What the hell?" and he took me to a restaurant literally half a block from my apartment, where he goes all the time. We drove there in his brand new penis car, a sporty white Porsche that still had the plastic on the seats and only something like thirty-seven miles on it. It may or may not have had a stick shift, I couldn't tell from his double-foot style of stop-and-go driving, but in the eight-block trip, I became extremely nauseous.

Over appetizers, he told me that he was sex-crazed and had a Ukrainian model whom he regularly fucked, but that he liked to go out on dates from the Lunch service because the ladies from the service were usually smarter. So far, I was his favorite because, not only was I smart, I was "hot," and I should see some of the homely ladies he had gotten stuck going out with. Suddenly I felt like a hooker.

But apparently I wasn't enough entertainment for Freddy, because he texted his friend to join us. That guy showed up within ten minutes, as if he'd been on call, and was also wearing a pink shirt. We made some small talk and by then I had had a few glasses of wine and some meatballs, and it was time to gracefully exit from the pink-shirt party. In retrospect, I don't know what the hell I was doing there in the first place. It was one of those nights when my daughter was at her dad's so I thought I'd stay out, regardless of the company. Freddy and I exchanged phone numbers and while I was using the ladies room (*read: on the toilet*) prior to leaving, Freddy texted me. I decided I would not respond at that point or later, and after a few texts, Freddy got the hint and eventually went away.

• • •

I knew that I'd made a mistake with the Lunch thing, but I was determined to get my money's worth. The next date I had from the scam service was with a different Freddy, fifty-one, at 7:00 p.m. (still too old a Freddy and still not lunch). This Freddy was described as a "tall, handsome, dapper" Wall Street guy. Are only Freddys available to a Madelyn?

This Freddy was tall all right, but a very awkward tall, like a deformed kind of seven feet tall with bad knees. He used to work in finance but was now a day trader out of his home in Connecticut, near where his Asian ex-wife lived with their Down Syndrome child, whom he never got to see because the Asian ex-wife had filed a restraining order after he stopped by her place unannounced one day. He reeled off all of the gory details of his dramatic life but was barely interested in my story and couldn't figure out the menu was also the placemat, which prompted him to be unnecessarily condescending to the waiter. I found him to be one of the most arrogant, self-centered, rude individuals I had ever met in my life. No wonder the Asian ex-wife wanted him to keep his distance. If I were to look at his situation sympathetically, however, it was actually kind of sad. The guy's arrogance was obviously a ruse for his insecurity. He clearly loved his son. His Asian ex did seem nuts the way he described her. I almost felt sorry for him when he said that he went on every date the Lunch ladies set up for him and he had been on something like eighty dates so far.

• • •

The next day, I told the scam service I wanted my money back. How dare they disrespect me so thoroughly and waste my time and money?

Freddy #1 had been forthcoming enough to let me know that he had stopped paying his membership fee but that the service's ratio of men to women was something like 20-80, so they continued to recycle the men whether or not they paid their fees. I challenged my "dating manager" with this accusation but she deflected it with a well-scripted response about how they have seven offices throughout the country and were totally reputable and it only takes one match and I should remain open-minded and I'm sure I tuned out because I have no idea what she said after that. But it was clear I wasn't getting my money back and Let's Do Lunch wasn't going to provide the solution to my loneliness.

I agreed to one more date before putting my membership on "hiatus" (*read: making them stop fixing me up with old guys and forfeiting my membership fee*). Fasil (not Freddy), I was told, was a doctor who worked at an Upper East Side hospital and was very handsome and well-traveled. I insisted that this lunch happen at lunchtime and put it in my calendar for three weeks from then—and promptly forgot all about it.

Three weeks later, I noticed the date on my calendar. I had already had my magical fourth date with Hector, where we talked for, like, six hours straight and slept together, and I was cautiously but surely falling for him. I almost canceled on this Fasil character, but then I thought what the hell? Realistically, and based on my past disasters, it was too soon to jump to hasty conclusions about Hector despite my feelings, so I reluctantly went to lunch, complete with pit in stomach.

I was running about fifteen minutes late to meet Dr. Fasil, but they don't provide you with any contact info for these blind dates, only the restaurant address. So I hustled and got there as fast as I could. I did toy with the idea of calling the restaurant and having them tell whatever guy that looked like he was waiting for me that I'd be there soon, but I figured fifteen minutes late (like Freddy #1) was acceptable. Borderline, but acceptable.

The place was a ghost town. There was no one at the desk when I first walked in so I said to a Pitbull-looking guy sitting at the bar, "Are you Fasil?" I was sort of hoping he was. At least he looked like Pitbull (the rapper, not the dog breed) and had some style, as opposed to the over-fifty, khaki-wearing Freddys.

"No," he said in an unidentifiable kind of sexy accent, "he's outside."

"How do you know? Do you work here?" I said.

"No, but there's some guy waiting outside."

I poked my head out the door but there was no one there. And there was no one else in the restaurant except two older ladies having lunch.

Finally, the host appeared. I think he might have also been the chef and maybe the waiter and busboy and probably the owner. He seemed quite frantic, despite fact that there was only one table seated. I told him my name and he found the reservation. He told me I was the first to arrive. "Phew!" I said to the maître d' guy in an attempt to lighten his serious mood, "I thought I was so late!"

The maître d' clearly picked up on my attempt to relax the situation and said at top volume, "OH YES! IT'S A DATE!!!!????" loud as fuck. The mysterious Pitbull guy clearly overheard and I was mortified.

As if I already didn't feel like there was a giant spotlight on me, he sat me smack in the center of the restaurant with nothing but empty tables all around me. I nervously read emails while this same guy kept refilling my ice-water glass and asking if I wanted to know the lunch specials. He pressured me to order some appetizers or a salad while I waited.

Time was ticking slowly. I didn't know where to direct my eyes. I sat up straight. I slouched. I read emails. I crossed my legs. I pretended to read more emails. Ten minutes passed. I pretended to send some emails. Fifteen minutes. Was Dr. Fasil going to be a no show?

The host-waiter-owner-chef-busboy kept trying to get me to order something. I could read his mind, "Lady, you're taking up a table in my empty restaurant." But I knew that as soon as I could officially call it a no show, I would want to race out the door and not have to deal with paying a bill, or anything that might remotely delay my exit.

I decided to kill some time in the ladies room so I sat on the toilet (two minutes), washed my hands (forty-five seconds) and reapplied my lipstick (twenty-two seconds). I took a few deep breaths. I talked to myself in the mirror, something along the lines of, "What the fuck are you doing you stupid bitch? Just leave now while you can."

At the stroke of twenty-nine minutes waiting time, I decided to officially give up. By the time I walked out the door and said thank you and good-bye to the host-waiter-owner-chef-busboy, it had officially been thirty minutes of waiting. Which was really forty-five minutes because I was fifteen minutes late.

I was so relieved I practically skipped home. I hadn't wanted to be there in the first place, and I took the whole thing as a sign that my instinct had been right. It had been a waste of time I could have used for something productive, but I felt liberated and good that the universe was confirming my instincts about Hector. Thank you, universe.

As I was flying out the door, feeling a lot lighter than when I walked in, Pitbull, who happened to be leaving right behind me, said, "That guy is crazy, by the way."

"Right? I shouldn't have to wait thirty minutes for some guy."

"You, lady, shouldn't have to wait five minutes for anyone."

• • •

I chewed the Lunch Ladies a new asshole the next day. Not only had I wasted valuable time and money with old Freddys, but now I had to deal with a no-show? They said that Dr. Fasil apologized profusely, something had come up with his important doctor job and he would love to reschedule. Well fuck that, I am sure he was sixty-five years old anyway. I demanded my money back, but the Lunch Bitches instead recommended the aforementioned "hiatus," after which I could renew my membership when I was ready to start dating again…" as if I were so crushed by Dr. No Show and too discouraged by the old Freddys that I needed time to regroup. Little did *they* know that I could have my soul fucked for free at any time I wanted. But the real fuck you to the Lunch Ladies was that I was on the verge of falling in love with someone else—for practically free, considering the three-month best value plan on DateABlackGuyWithAJobDotCom was a fraction of the cost of the Scam Lunch Service.

CHAPTER 14

HH AND HEROIN

One night, an artist I was working with was performing at a nice venue in lower Manhattan called City Winery. I invited Hector to join me for the show and when we got there, David Johansen from the New York Dolls, also known as Buster Poindexter, was at the entrance. I had put David on the guest list myself because he was a friend of my artist, but the idiot with the clipboard was giving him a hard time. In a valiant attempt to be Buster Poindexter's hero and impress Hector at the same time, I swooped in and told the clipboard girl who I was and who *he* was. "Let him in!" I demanded with my record label authority, and she did. I reintroduced myself to David/ Buster and reminded him that we had worked together on the last New York Dolls album. He just glared at me. Crickets. Sheesh, it wasn't my fault it was a shitty album that sold five copies.

Hector found all this very amusing and told me that he had a David Johansen story, too. When that last album had been released, about eight years earlier, he was hired to be the photographer at the band's in-store performance at the old Tower Records on 4th and Broadway. He was conspicuously the only black guy in the entire place of about three hundred rock 'n' roll fans, but that's not the point.

"What?! I put that event together!" I said. That in-store had been one of my first initiatives at my new job. "If you were hired as the photographer, that means someone on my staff hired you!" The world can't be that small. Hector immediately whipped out his iPhone and searched the web for photos he had shot at the event. Sure enough, in the pixilated background, you could see someone who might have been me standing in the spot where I remember standing. I wasn't positive it was me. My hair looked weirdly teased up or else my head was an odd shape. And who was I standing next to? About a week later, Hector dug up the high-resolution version of the photo and, lo and behold, there was no mistaking me. The bouffant was actually sunglasses on top of my head and I was standing next to someone from the label who I barely knew.

That photo had been taken in the summer of 2006, and looking back at myself, I realized that it captured a moment just prior to my entire life upheaval. I had just begun a new job, my husband was just about to leave me, my mother would be dead before the end of the year, and my sister would follow her shortly thereafter.

Hector and I decided that the universe had put us together on that day but then realized the timing wasn't right. We both needed to live our stories separately before we could come together eight years later. We both believed this. We were falling in love.

I had joined the DateABlackGuyWithAJobDotCom website on September 10th and Hector and I had our first date on September 16th. How could I be so lucky? How could this have been so easy? I didn't want to fuck up my shot at happiness and permanence, but, given my history, I was afraid it wasn't real. Can you blame me?

Chloe applied some tough love. "No more blind dates. No more meaningless hookups. NO MORE," she warned. "Don't fuck it up, hooker."

Email from Chloe:

Put your attention into MrHH and see what happens! If it all falls apart, which I'm sure it won't, then you can go back to being a total slut.

:)

I so didn't want to go back to being a total slut—that was the whole point. But one doesn't reform her ways in one short month. It takes time, y'see. And it also takes time to analyze *why* one behaves like such a slut. If I could get to the bottom of that, maybe I could address the underlying issues. I had moments of brief clarity about it, like while on the treadmill or in the shower, but if I didn't write down the revelation at the very moment I had it, I would conveniently forget what it was, thereby pushing my deep-seated issues farther away to avoid dealing with them. That's normal, right? We've already ascertained that I like sex and I'm looking for love; and this combination led to slut-like behavior. But now that I was seeing someone, why was I having trouble accepting the possibility of real love—and the necessity for monogamy that might accompany that?

OK, here's a reason. A big one. Because I am so deathly afraid of rejection. Rejection now or rejection later. Big rejection or small rejection. All kinds of rejection. I am terrified of it. The short-term variety stings but the worst kind is the rejection that comes after years of being with someone. I knew this firsthand. Both my ex-husband and MD had rejected me after I had invested considerably in those relationships. How could I possibly endure another life-shattering rejection?

I think the fear-of-rejection thing is why I had a hard time letting go of other men in the early stages of dating Hector. I was afraid that he'd eventually reject me and that I'd have wasted another X number of precious, fuckable years I had left on yet another bad investment.

So, I didn't eliminate any of the others outright. I wasn't sleeping with anyone else (*read: fucking*), but I didn't tell any of them I was seeing someone, either. I still got "hey u" or "are you in NY?" or "Hi, what are you up to?" texts from the usual cast of characters, but Soul-Fucker-Who-Shall-Not-Be-Named would be the most difficult one to quit.

I ignored some of the texts or responded indifferently, but I wasn't actually closing any doors. I did, however, remove my profile from DateABlackGuy. Hector and I hadn't discussed exclusivity at this point, but maybe it was supposed to be understood. I was ready. I was beginning to feel ready, willing, and able to overcome my rejection fears and forsake all others. I couldn't wait to do that, frankly.

• • •

Kevin, though.

I had to have Kevin. Just once. This flirtation had been brewing for almost a year, so I had to have him at least once. Once. Honest. No, really. Just once with Kevin, and then I'd be done.

I had met Kevin at, of all places, my daughter's gym. No fitness facility is sacred, apparently. My daughter trains in mixed martial arts and when I dropped her off at the gym for the first time, I decided this is where I was going to find a man. There were so many fantastic contenders—but after researching and snooping, I learned they were all way too young for me. Not only that, but none were out to meet women at the gym because they were all too serious about their training. Boring.

However, one very special young man caught my eye. I distinctly remember the moment I first saw him. He was standing at the front desk checking in and behind him, the sun shining through the window was casting a magical glow, simultaneously silhouetting and illuminating him like an angel who descended from Jiu Jitsu Heaven to fuck me.

I was like a heroin addict and Kevin was the little bit of stash I had left before getting clean. He was top-notch, high quality stuff, the absolute best. I couldn't let it go to waste. So I'd just finish this last bit off and then I'd be done. Honest. I promised myself this would be the last of it…and then I'd go to rehab. Promise.

CHAPTER 15

DEAR TYRONE

Email to Chloe:

Let me ask you something. When you make plans with someone on a fourth date to go on a trip to Vancouver together (it's on, flights booked), do you assume that you're seeing each other exclusively? I mean, maybe. Maybe not. This was never discussed, and damned if I'm going to be the one to bring it up.

So when the other brothas are circling around asking to see you...the cop, the flight attendant, the trainer(s), HMN, and of course Kevin...do you just blow them off? Shut them down? Continue to date them? Keep them hanging on? I honestly don't even want to bother to see anyone, but I don't want to close any doors in case Hector is not who Hector currently appears to be.

Any advice? They're all fucking hitting me up today for some reason.

Let's pause and ruminate on the key phrase here for a moment: "*... **in case Hector isn't who Hector currently*** *appears to be*." Virtually no one whom I have loved or tried to love in the recent past turned out to be who they appeared to be. No one. Let's recap:

- **Husband** – If a happy, glorious seven-year marriage to your best friend isn't sacred, then what is?
- **MD** – There was shady behavior and red flags from the beginning, followed by hidden truths and signals that I ignored for five long years. To this day, I don't know what was fake and what was real about him.
- **Dele** – To his credit, he never represented himself as anything but an asshole from day one. So that WAS real, even if I chose to ignore the reality. He was a REAL asshole. But perhaps he's disqualified anyway, since I never loved him.
- **Fuck Buddies & Trainers** – In the *Fuck Buddy Handbook*, it is fair game to slightly misrepresent yourself and your intentions in order to get laid. Am I any different from them? As far as love goes, I *loved* that I was lucky enough to enjoy those stunning, perfect, and gorgeous bodies. It was the ultimate in manifesting my ego's deepest desires: They were fantasies come to life. In each case, though, I was probably hoping secretly that a real relationship would magically manifest. Then, I woke up and realized none of it was real.
- **Soul Fucker** – He was and remains simply the sexiest man on earth—straight up fact. Real. There will be no other who will ever compare. Real. As real as it gets, the pure, unbridled and undeniable attraction.

That's real as fuck. But, he was and remains pretty much totally unavailable. Ergo: unreal.

- **The Mysterious Kevin** – He was one of those inspirational- quote posters on Instagram; Mixed-Boy27 was his handle. In his defense, this was prior to the inspiration-quote posting craze. He was very early on that tip, so it seemed to me that he was revealing deep thoughts, his pure soul, and emotions. He was a walking broken heart, wounded by the past much like myself, except that his past was considerably shorter than mine as he was twenty-ish years my junior. (This is a record for me, stick a feather in my cap!) But I wanted to identify with him, relate to him, and help him with my years of experience. We definitely had a connection and seemed to be searching for similar things. But once I faced up to our phenomenal age difference, the whole thing became absurd. Absurdity is also not real. Hot, but not real. Which brings us to...

- **Hector** – So, what about Hector? Real or unreal? I was afraid to explore the question on paper for fear of jinxing the possibilities, but Hector did seem real. The epitome of real. If Hector was who he appeared to be, I would believe he was answering my *Dear Tyrone* letter.

What's a *Dear Tyrone letter*, you ask? Doesn't every woman have their version of a *Dear Tyrone* letter? It's the letter you're supposed to write to your ideal mate. The act of writing it will miraculously bring your soul mate to you.

My letter is to Tyrone, of course, but yours is probably to William or Michael or maybe Shlomo or Antonio or, maybe Janice. Whoever. Here are some excerpts from my *Dear Tyrone* letter:

> I've been everywhere before we found each other, searching, exploring, testing, experimenting, hoping, considering all options. I don't require much, I am very self-sufficient. But I have been missing real love for many years. I'm not a slut, I'm just looking for love. OK, yeah, maybe I behave like a slut sometimes, but I am really just on a quest for love and loyal friendship.
>
> You're probably younger than I am (about ten years, I hope), because I can't bear to be around men my own age. I promise that as a couple, people will think we're the same age because we are equally fit and youthful.
>
> We will make time to spend together, squeezing it into our busy lives. It may be a challenge, but valuing each other's independence is key. I have a big job. I am not sure which big job it is when we meet, but I'm sure it eats up much of my time. I love my work, it has consumed much of my life since long before you came along, so thank you for accepting it as a part of me.
>
> Thank you for laughing at my jokes and getting me. Yes, I can be foul and crude, but I am honest and real and just going for the laugh. I was not always quite as transparent in other

relationships (i.e. ones that I didn't want to be in), but with you, I'm in it to win it and there is no bullshit.

I will always feel safe and not afraid that you're going to leave me like the others did. If I ever need something or am scared, you will be there. I don't have this aching emptiness anymore. You've filled it. The formerly omnipresent deep, vacuous sadness is now gone. You're my man. I no longer fear abandonment. I can exhale.

Thanks for fixing that drawer that never closed, the doorknob that always fell off, the light switch, the loose cabinet, and all the other odds and ends that we two girls living together always just shrugged off. You fixed it. You fixed everything.

Do you exist? If so, can you please show up sooner rather than later so I don't waste any more time with other guys?

Thanks.

Love,

Me

I so wanted to believe that Hector was real. I had such high hopes. But how was I ever supposed to believe it? I guess the answer was that I couldn't not try (a double negative, which I don't not want to use). I couldn't be so afraid of more heartbreak that I didn't even try. I would just have to open myself up to it, and allow myself to be vulnerable.

There. I had said it. I was not going to be afraid anymore. I had hoped to be able to share these feelings with Hector some day, when they might even seem trivial and unimportant because everything would be as it should. My previous life, and all of the men who came (and came) in and out (and in and out) of it, wouldn't amount to more than a distant memory and silly fodder for emails to Chloe.

On the other hand, because there is always the dark side, *if Hector wasn't who Hector appeared to be*, I might just give up entirely.

I'm rooting for you, MrHH. I am really rooting for you.

CHAPTER 16

GLASS BALLS

(Not *those* kind of balls. Get your mind out of the gutter for five minutes and let me tell a nice story.)

There was a time when I lived in the South Pacific with my family. At this point, everyone immediately asks the same question: "Was your father in the military?" No, he worked for an engineering firm contracted by the government to conduct missile testing in the Pacific Ocean in the sixties and seventies. In other words, they were pretending to blow shit up.

My large family of seven shared a small trailer in the residential area (*read: trailer park*) of the one-mile-long island in the Kwajalein Atoll. We lived there on three separate occasions, for a little more than a year each time. These experiences left an indelible mark on all of my family members. We each have our own romanticized versions of our life on "Kwaj"; the island's beauty, mystery, and simplicity, and how it affected each of us. As for me, I'll never love another beach as much as I did the tiny, quiet, private, pristine Emon Beach, which I still believe belongs to me. Everyone else is just borrowing it.

Each time we returned to the "mainland," we brought trunks full of souvenirs. Our house was filled with monkey-pod wood serving sets, coral sculptures, household items made of shells and palm stalks, and other Polynesian- and Samoan-flavored trinkets. My favorites weren't from the one and only store on the island (called Macy's, though it was more like a Woolworth's), they were souvenirs from the boundless Pacific Ocean herself. Glass balls from Japanese fishing boats would often wash up on the rocky beaches of the atoll's cliff side and were collected by the island's residents.

The glass balls originated in Japan, made by the Hokyuro Glass company, and were used to support the nets cast by Japanese trawlers fishing for King Crabs off the Bering sea coast of the Aleutian islands. Sometimes a ball would break loose from a net and drift for thousands of miles in the Japanese current. By the time it reached the beach of Kwajalein, it had probably been drifting for at least ten years. My family shipped back about a dozen of them and we siblings divvied them up. I ended up with three, dropped and broke one (they were heavy, about 24" in diameter of thick glass), and kept two in storage.

One day early on in the Hector Honeymoon phase, when rummaging through my storage locker, I discovered the glass balls. They had been collecting dust and serving no purpose in storage, so I thought it might be nice to clean them up and display them in my apartment. I asked Hector to help me carry them upstairs as I recounted my fading memories of that magical island. Hector said he wondered about how much turmoil those glass balls must have endured during those ten years, and how miraculous it is that they survived and were saved.

I thought Hector and I were like two of those glass balls, bouncing around alone in the salty ocean for years with no clear direction, no protection from the harsh elements, and no anchor. We'd finally landed on a beautiful and peaceful beach, finally safe. Together.

CHAPTER 17

MIXED BOY

It was November and I had been dating Hector steadily for about two months. I hadn't been seeing anyone else. I was happy. I thought I might even be falling in love. We took that trip to Vancouver, which was romantic, adventurous, action-packed and sex-packed. We talked incessantly, shared stories, drove, walked, toured, ate, drank wine, and really connected in a deep way.

Hector had been talking about introducing me to his mother and his brother, who lived close to each other on the Upper East Side, but I hadn't even seen his apartment yet, which kind of bothered me. He lived in Astoria, Queens, but right after I met him, he'd moved out of his apartment because some roof repair work was being done. He'd been staying with his brother and when I asked him when he might be moving back home, he didn't seem to know. The fact that I had no idea where or how he lived was the one thing missing from our otherwise beautifully blossoming relationship. I would think that around the two-month mark of a new and steady relationship would be the time you might expect to see more deeply into your partner's life. Being invited to see someone's home seemed like a reasonable enough request. It might even be the time to start meeting each other's relatives, friends, offspring, and possibly the superintendent. The fact that Hector's apartment was still a dark mystery just didn't sit right with me.

But Hector spoke so often about introducing me to his family that I thought maybe I was being overly suspicious, making too big a deal about not having seen his under-construction apartment way the fuck out in Queens. Why did it matter so much to me? I think I was still carrying around MD baggage, assuming that anything that isn't immediately verifiable or visible to me must be a lie or a ruse of some kind. I knew I needed to get over that mistrust of trivial things, but a girl has a gut feeling sometimes.

Hector told me that when he'd told his mother about me, she'd said, "You seem so happy" (en Español, because apparently she spoke no English, which Hector said wouldn't be a problem when we met, because she would still like me a lot even if we couldn't communicate), to which he replied, "I am." That was nice to know, because for the first time in ages, I was feeling pretty happy myself, and I decided to ignore my spidey-sense of suspicion.

But *fuck*. I still had this stash of heroin I hadn't used yet. It was just a little bit, so I wanted to finish it up and then head to rehab, like I promised. (Rehab being that I'd stop dicking around and dedicate myself to being a one-man woman.) The budding relationship with Hector was what I had wanted for a long time, so how could I be so stupid and risk fucking it up? But then again, even though

Hector and I were feeling like a couple, it had only been two months, after all. We were both fiercely independent and lived very separate, very busy lives. Even though there was another toothbrush in my bathroom, the talk of meeting family was just talk. We hadn't even had the "we are exclusive" conversation. Maybe that was just supposed to be understood? Or not. Why didn't he bring it up? And why was I so afraid to bring it up? Maybe because it had only been two months and I was afraid of scaring him off, so I kept my mouth shut and tried not to make any assumptions.

• • •

This is what I told myself in a cab heading home after a work-related dinner, after which I was to meet Mixed Boy at my apartment so that we could "drink, talk, and get to know each other better." The drinking and talking didn't last very long; soon we were naked, sweaty, and hanging from the light fixtures. He was a superbly gorgeous human being, his body young, hard, and strong. His fingers were long and sexy and clean. His nose was perfection and his lips were beautifully shaped, tender, and sexy. I traced his tattoos with my tongue and admired every square inch of his dark caramel, hair-free, perfect skin. We had passionate, warm, loving, violent, and hot sex for hours and hours until I was so tired I couldn't do it anymore. He snored for a little while, then got up and left around 8:00 am, claiming that he hadn't slept at all.

We never said anything about seeing each other again. He was twenty-seven years old. I think I am older than his mother, whom he told me was thinking about having another baby.

The heroin was all gone now. That was the last of it. It was really good stuff, though. I wouldn't mind having had a just a little more, actually.

No! I said I would check myself into rehab, so that's what I was going to do. Buuuuuut if he happened to text me...NO! NO, NO, NO. Bad girl! No more heroin. Seriously, I quit. No joke. That was it. Honest. I was done. Really. It was so good. But no.

CHAPTER 18

UNTITLED

Trying to write a book is fucking hard. As a book *reader,* which is what I assume you are, since you've gotten this far, you must know this. It's a long process and a fuckload of work. You can't do it alone either, you need friends and editors and enemies to tell you whether you're on the right track or not. If you are, you have a fuck-ton of work to do. If you're not, well, you have even more work to do. Every writer has his or her own process, and as I was figuring out mine, I began collecting and archiving some of my emails to Chloe. After all, it was Chloe who gave me the idea of recounting my stories in greater detail when she said, "Your shit is so funny, I'm going to start a blog for you so the whole world will know how wack you are."

Based on her reactions to my emails, I thought maybe some of my antics might be worth elaborating on—certainly not for posterity (eww), but because there just might be a few women out there who were equally confident in their sexuality but just as confused about their paths. Maybe they'd read my stories and go, "YES! I KNOW WHAT YOU MEAN!!" Maybe one of them would send me an email or a fan letter kind of thing and we'd become pen pals because we have so much in common and can relate to each other without judgment. And then maybe another woman would do that, too, and then I'd have a few like-minded friends (or pen pals) and none of us would feel quite so alone anymore. That, and also I would like to make someone else laugh besides Chloe.

Anyway, during my Super Slut Summer, as I told my stories to Chloe via email, I wasn't yet preparing any of the introductions to characters or context or editorializing. I was just taking bits and pieces of our emails and adding some stream-of-consciousness soul-searching diary entries that weren't meant to be funny. I was starting to cobble together some ideas for chapters. I changed some details, and some names were (slightly) changed, too, but if any of those motherfuckers decide to read this book, they will know exactly who they are. But you, my special new friend, won't. And that's the point.

I did a lot of cutting and pasting of the emails and of my diary entries into various Word docs that I titled something that would let me know what or whom it was about, such as "Lunch Bitch" or "The Nigerian." Sometimes I pasted random thoughts or one-off ideas into a doc I called "Notes to Incorporate," which was exactly that. I was a cutting-and-pasting fiend.

I kept this collection of Word docs in a handy folder on my desktop called *Untitled*. In my mind, the collection wasn't ready for a title; it was too undercooked. It certainly wasn't meant for anyone to see yet—if ever. Diarrhea of the fingers is not funny. I'm not witty or charming in any way until I put some effort into forming cohesive thoughts that flow together, all in the same font. Also, the raw data was deeply personal and borderline embarrassing.

Then, Hector discovered it.

• • •

I'd made a big decision! I was finally making the move from PC to Mac. My PC laptop was getting long in the tooth (a technical term that I learned from an IT guy) and I was due for an upgrade.

Those Apple Store employees sure do make you feel like they're your best friends. My personal Apple sales professional was so understanding and sweet I thought we might be on a date. He asked me about my needs and desires, he understood me and was willing to help me through this transition and patiently answer all my questions. Because I was sure that my Apple boyfriend (I didn't catch his name) had my back, I had no doubt that the transition from PC to Mac would be seamless. I would simply drop off my PC to him and forty-eight to seventy-two hours later, return to pick up my new Mac. All of my files and programs would be sucked off of my old PC and magically transferred onto my new Mac and it would be fully operable. My Apple boyfriend said so and I believed him.

When I returned seventy-two hours later (of course it wasn't the lesser option), my Apple BF was nowhere to be found. An Apple Stranger explained that there had been a problem with the conversion; that my new Mac wasn't able to read from my PC.

But where was my Apple BF? I was sure *he* could help me. Was it his day off??

The Apple Stranger said I would have to do some elaborate thing, like transfer everything from the PC to an external hard drive and then import it from there onto the Mac. Zzzzzzzzzzz. Oh, sorry, I dozed off because this is really fucking boring, but there is a point, I promise.

Hector was with me when I went to pick up the Mac, and thankfully, he is a Mac wizard. (Remember, he Photoshops for a living.) He suggested that instead of buying the $250 giant hard drive the Apple Stranger was trying to sell me, we borrow one from his office and come right back. Having already spent a small fortune on this endeavor, I was all for saving a few bucks.

How exciting! I was going to see Hector's office! This felt like some kind of big step for me. I still hadn't seen his home because of that mysterious roof repair work, and I hadn't met his family or friends yet, either. So, this door crack opening felt significant. It wasn't like I was going to meet any of his coworkers, since it was a Saturday, but at least I'd get a little peek into his world.

It turned out to be uneventful and major at the same time. His office was just as he'd described it to me; there were no framed photos of a wife or kids, or anything suspicious or inexplicable. After a quick office tour, we picked up a hard drive, hopped back on the subway, and headed back to Apple.

It seemed easy enough. Suck all the shit off the PC onto the hard drive and then suck it off the hard drive onto the Mac. We were going to do it at the Apple store so that if any problems came up, we'd be among the Geniuses who could help.

Everything seemed to work fine. Hector was furiously clicking around my new Mac desktop like a pro...opening things, clicking things, testing things, more clicking. Then, in his mad, speed-demon clicking frenzy, he opened the folder on my desktop called *Untitled*.

I am sure my sudden and extreme reaction of "**NO NO NO NOOOOOOOO!!!**" must have raised an eyebrow. "**Close that folderrrrr!!!**" (read in echoey, dramatic, slow-motion voice). But it was too late. The folder was open and all my private Word file titles were visible, such as:

Why Am I Such A Slut?
Date A Black Guy With A Job
Fuck Buddies
Every One Of These Trainers is So Fucking Hot
Hot Mixed Boy
Big Black Cock
Dear Tyrone
and...
MrHH

I felt as if Hector had opened my diary and a huge piece of my secret soul was exposed. I reached over him and closed the folder as fast as I could without really knowing what, if anything, Hector saw. He was so soft-spoken and even-keeled that I couldn't gauge his reaction. I felt sweaty and nervous and shaky, but we just continued on with the PC-to-Mac transition as if nothing had happened. So maybe nothing had happened. This is what I went with.

Once the transition was complete, Hector took the hard drive with him, volunteering that he would delete all the files and wipe it clean before returning it to work. I asked him for confirmation on that, as there were work files, confidential stuff, personal finances, and my daughter's files on there. Of course he understood and assured me all would be deleted. I didn't have any reason to believe otherwise. I trusted Hector.

I had intentionally not set up a password on my new computer at the Apple store, either. This was because I had spent years in Corporate America where, every time I got up to pee and came back to my desk, I'd have to re-enter my password seventeen times. I don't know why anyone thought our stupid music business information was so valuable. Who cared if someone hacked into my computer and got Gene Simmons' address and phone number or access to the Nickelback marketing budget? I mean, I know that hating Nickelback* is like a sport now, so maybe someone actually *would* be interested in that, but hello, not the point.

I also didn't create a computer password to show Hector I had nothing to hide, despite what he may have seen when he was clicking around like a madman. Actually, I did have a lot to hide, but I didn't think I would have to actually *hide* it. I wasn't ready for any deep confessions just yet.

I felt happy that my man had helped me with this major tech transition. I had to carry both the PC and the Mac home from the Apple store, and he helped me do that, too. This is what boyfriends are for, I thought. *I have a boyfriend.*

Don't hate Nickelback. They're lovely men. All the teasing and ribbing is akin to bullying and it's not a good look, nor is it funny, so grow up and stop it or go pick on someone your own size.

CHAPTER 19

HAPPY NEW YEAR

New Year's Eve is weird. I never really know what to do. Each year figuring that out is a new challenge depending on who I'm hanging out with, whether or not my daughter is home, or if I'm in NYC or not. Lord knows I've had my fair share of New Year's Eve experiences, running the gamut from scoring cocaine at 2:00 a.m. to dozing off on my couch alone at 11:15 with my kid asleep in the other room.

This year, I decided to host a small party for a handful of close friends and family. My brother and his wife were in town, my sister came in from Philly, and my old college roommate and oldest (or should I say longest-term?) friend, her husband, and two kids were in town from Connecticut. My upstairs neighbor, another close friend of Louise's, would also join us, and *he* is actually my *oldest* friend, so I had fun with making those introductions. Rounding out the crowd was my crew of cousins, one of whom has the world's greatest nickname: Sloppy Balls (a word play on his first and last name), my daughter, and of course Hector. Hector was going to be part of my New Year's Eve celebration with my closest friends and family. That's some serious couple shit. Happy Fucking New Year to me.

The day before the party, I had lots to do: planning menus, figuring out seating arrangements, making lists of party supplies, food, drinks, and don't forget ice. Imogen and I jumped in the car and went to Target with a long shopping list. I realized while we were there that I hadn't heard back from Hector about whether or not he was bringing brussels sprouts so that we could make the special recipe we'd discovered together when cooking like a happy, domestic couple in my kitchen a few weeks earlier.

So, before leaving the Target parking lot, I texted him, "Hi, baby. Is everything ok? Haven't heard back from you, are you ok?"

I am not one to badger a person. If I don't hear from you I assume you are busy, sick, out of battery, dead, otherwise occupied, or uninterested. Some guys have accused me of making them "chase" me because I tend to be uncommunicative. But I don't believe it is dignified for a woman to chase a man, as archaic as that may sound coming from a modern ho like myself. You already know how I feel, you know I expect to hear from you, so, I don't chase. That "Hello, is everything OK" text translated to, "You haven't texted me back about the brussels sprouts in more than 24 hours so I can only assume you are deathly ill or something is horribly wrong because not responding to a brussels sprout text in that amount of time while we are clearly in an intimate, exclusive, and loving relationship is kind of uncool. I am not a needy bitch so I won't call you out on it, but 'is everything ok' should be enough of a message for you to know that your silence about brussels sprouts or any other matter of equal or similar importance is not cool."

Five hours later, I got this response:

Hey Madelyn. I was at work yesterday and found the hard drive that we used for your computer. There were still some of your files on it, so I deleted all of them except for one called MrHH. It was a big mistake, but I read it and I didn't realize that you were still seeing other men. I don't want to go on and on about it here, but obviously I don't feel too good about what I read.

PUUUUUUUKE. OMG. Jesus, Lord help me. What the fuck? Oh holy shit holy shit holy shit.

The first thing I did was immediately call him. This was ridiculous. A complete and total misunderstanding, I just needed to explain that whatever he read was just the rantings of a lunatic, out of context. I was sure I could explain. What could he possibly have read that made him think I was seeing other men? The MrHH doc was about how I was falling for him and I was just a little scared... wasn't that all it said? Fuck, I needed to read it ASAP. As I was frantically trying to call him, I was thinking all of this and his phone kept going straight to voice mail. Voice mail. Voice mail. Voice mail. Jesus.

I texted him:

Please don't ignore me. I need to talk to you and explain. You know that I am working on writing a book, and what you read is totally out of context. Please don't jump to inaccurate conclusions.

I dashed over to the computer to read what he read. Oh FUUUUUCK. This is horrible. It starts out great...gushing about MrHH and how I'm falling for him and how it seems too good to be true but that I am not sure about where it is leading and I'm a little afraid. All of that is fine, even though a little embarrassing and showing my vulnerability—but at least it's nice and truthful. Then, at the bottom of that document, I had pasted this email to Chloe:

> The trainers should be off limits at this point for so many reasons, right? But mostly because it's not truly fulfilling, it's like my addiction. HDT texted me yesterday saying, "Got time for me today?" and I said "No, I have a meeting this morning." I didn't even think "No, I can't be with you anymore." In my brain I was like LITERALLY, "No, I have a meeting."
>
> Then today, Soul Fucker texted me, and you know I can't resist him, so he came over for a quick blow job. What is wrong with me?

I *can* explain. This incriminating cut/paste was from an earlier time, during my MD relationship. No, seriously, it was. As you can clearly see from the font change, it was not part of my thoughts about MrHH. For some unknown reason, I cut/pasted that particular email onto the bottom of the MrHH document. What I *can't* explain is exactly why I did that. But I think it was the early draft of the chapter that you just read about Mixed Boy. When writing about MrHH, I was aware that I was falling for him and it was clear in what I had written. But I was simultaneously trepidatious about where we were headed and whether or not we were exclusive. There was something about juxtaposing deep, vulnerable thoughts of falling in love with giving a hot trainer a quick blow job that was funny to me. It *is* kind of funny. Come on.

I texted Hector again.

Why are you ignoring me? Let's talk. I need to explain.

Nothing. A few more attempts at a phone call, still voice mail, voice mail, and voice mail. Two long hours went by while I was trying to put shit together for the party and what the fuck? Who launches a text like that and then disappears? Is this really the way he deals with conflict? Just disappears? This is not good at all. It was obvious to Chloe, too.

Text to Chloe:

MM: Emergency! Emergency! Hector read some shit on my computer about Soul Fucker and blow jobs and he is now ignoring me and won't pick up the phone or text me back so I can't even try to explain. I am freaking the fuck out. What do I do???!!!

CHLOE: Oh fuck ma, that's crazy. How did this happen? What do you mean he read shit

on your computer? And why is he ignoring you? I'm sorry, but that sounds like a bigger problem.

I was now getting paranoid that he might not have deleted everything except the MrHH document, as he claimed. Maybe had he read some of the other files. If that was the case, then I would have to explain a lot more than just my cutting-and-pasting strategy. I'd have to tell him more about my past—and who I really am—and I wasn't ready to do that yet. We were only three months into our relationship, and while I was willing and able to tell the ugly truth eventually, I didn't think it needed to be so soon, on demand, under these circumstances.

I *was* in love with Hector so I decided I'd do whatever it took to clear up this misunderstanding.

After making me sweat, puke, shake, and shiver for at least three hours, he finally returned my call. His voice was calm and quiet, ready to listen. Mine was shaky, desperate.

"You know that I am trying to write a book, right? What you read was not meant for anyone to read, let alone you. And hopefully you also saw that I wrote some really nice things about you and our relationship…"

"Yes, I did, and I appreciate that. But I also read that you gave someone a blow job in your apartment."

"Yes but that was way earlier. Before you. That was a cut-and-paste from an old email. You can tell because the fonts are different. Did you notice that? That stuff was from a whole different time! Baby, I haven't been with anyone else since we have been together."

Silence.

"Look. I admit that I come with a past, doesn't everyone have a past? OK, so maybe mine is a bit sordid, but I assure you that whatever you read was totally out of context. My notes aren't chronological and besides, that stuff is just in there for shock value, for entertainment's sake. For the *book*. Once I finish all the stories and put them in order, it will all make sense. Please don't take what you read as a literal account of anything that happened since we met."

Silence.

"Hector. You know me, right? I'm the person you know and love. Not the person who wrote those notes for a book that doesn't even exist yet."

"Yes, I think I know you."

"You do, Hector! You know me. What you read is not me. This is me, here on the phone. Please trust that. I need you to trust me."

"I want to trust you, Madelyn."

"Good! I'm so happy to hear that. You can."

Silence.

"So…are we OK?"

Silence.

"Listen, I'll explain more when I see you. Are you still coming over?"

"I don't think that's a good idea. I don't want anything to feel awkward. I'll just stay at my mom's tonight. I hope your party is good. Bye."

• • •

I painted on a smile with lip liner and hosted the worst New Year's Eve party ever.

Everyone was gone by 11:00 p.m., thank God. My brother and his wife thought it was a good idea to walk over to Times Square for the midnight ball drop, despite my warnings that they would never get close, they would freeze to death while trying, or, if not, certainly get trampled to death by the crowds. The Connecticut family was up way past their kids' bed times and these kids are on like a military-style schedule. My sister tagged along with my brother and wife. And the Balls families all wanted to go have sex, I guess. So, my kid and I were left to clean up and watch New Year's Rockin' Eve together. At midnight, I rang in the new year with my girl, my best pal and trusty companion, by my side, making me laugh hysterically about something super silly despite the fact that I felt like I died inside.

Once Imogen was asleep I cried for almost an hour, which is big because I'm not really a crier. If I lost Hector to this stupid snafu, I would officially give up on men. This was the most promising relationship I'd had since my ex-husband. I whispered promises to Hector, to myself, to the universe, to my angels, to all my dead friends and relatives. I swore that if I could just have another opportunity with Hector, I would give the relationship my all. I would never cheat on him. I would be faithful and I would be honest. I would even, as impossible as I believed it would be to do, permanently quit Soul Fucker. This was a loud wake up call and I was heeding the fuck out of it.

The next day, I got a text from Hector that said, "Happy New Year. Here's to a great new year together." It included

a photo of us as a happy couple on our Vancouver trip.

"Happy New Year to you too, baby," I wrote back. "Look how happy we are in that photo. I can't wait to make more memories with you like that."

The next thing I got was some heart emojis, a thumbs up, and maybe a smiley face, so I knew everything would be OK. It was a new year, indeed, but there was no need to make resolutions. I already knew what they would be.

CHAPTER 20

TRIPS TO FLORIDA
(READ IN KANYE "FLASHING LIGHTS" VOICE)

Email from Chloe:

Damn, girl. You take more vacations than anyone I know. How do you have time to take all these trips? Am I going to have to start a travel section in your blog? When is your ass and MrHH coming out here?

Once we'd determined that we were travel-compatible, Hector and I couldn't book flights fast enough. We took a trip to Miami and stayed in my favorite beachfront hotel. We went to Tobago (his homeland), and he took me to his favorite beachfront property, a special spot where he used to vacation with his family. We took a trip to LA and stayed with Chloe and her fiancé, Luke. I couldn't wait for Chloe to meet Hector, feeling that this would somehow validate our relationship. Though it wasn't the purpose of the trip, hanging with Chloe was fortunate because she and Luke would be getting married a few months later and, of course, Hector would be my date to the wedding.

We both genuinely loved to travel. I had an old-school paper world map on which we marked the places each of us had already been in different colors (red for me and green for him; the colors of our respective suitcases–puke), then we highlighted the places we wanted to go together in yellow.

We already had a plan to go to Ojai, California for Chloe's wedding. After that, we were going to hit Montreal (a city I didn't feel the need to visit again, but Hector loved it and wanted to experience it with me, so I agreed to go, to be a nice girlfriend). He also suggested another trip to Tobago, but this time it would include a visit to Trinidad, where he has family, for his birthday. Hector also wanted me to tag along on some of his upcoming work-related trips to Washington DC and the Sundance and Toronto Film Festivals. I would be headed for gold status on United Airlines.

The universe's timing may have been off eight years ago, at the New York Dolls' in-store appearance, but the Online Dating Gods seemed to have made up for it by connecting us quickly and efficiently. Neither of us had to renew our trial memberships on DateA-BlackGuyWithAJobDotCom.

The marketing people at DateABlackGuyWithA-JobDotCom should make us their poster couple and do a little profile on us, I thought. "Look how easy it is! True interracial love can happen for you, too." Our success story would be the first thing you saw when you clicked on the home page, complete with our fabulous smiling photo that reflected our supreme happiness and the obligatory sappy quote. We could even be the ambassadors for the site and go on speaking tours and press trips. Our message would be: *Don't be afraid of online dating. What's meant to be will be, so have faith, girls! Don't give up, guys! True love can happen to anyone! Just shell out $29.95 and you too can be as happy as this fabulous-looking, nausea-inducing interracial couple on the home page.*

• • •

This is the part of the book where you stop and ask yourself, "Why are there still so many more pages left?" You may be thinking:

- "She found her man; what gives?"
- "Is the rest of this book just about her happy relationship? Gross."
- "Does he move in or something? Since that Queens apartment probably doesn't even exist?"
- "I thought this was a sex book. I want to read more steamy stories."
- "Why has she still not seen that apartment? Does he have a wife and kids there or something?"
- "Does Charlie Brown know she has a 'boo' now?"
- Or more likely,
- "She probably fucks it up, dumb slut."

Just keep fucking reading, bitches.

CHAPTER 21

#CHLOE'S LAST COCK

Email from Chloe:
> Hey lady, Lucky [Luke's nickname] and I would love for you to give a toast at our wedding. What do you think? We both think that you would do an amazing job. No need to stress or make a big deal out of it, just be your usual funny self, no pressure!
> Loves you,
> C-Lo

Being asked to be a "main bitch" at Chloe's wedding was a great honor. She also asked me to help organize her bachelorette party in Miami. I couldn't have been more flattered. C-Lo's ragtag, eclectic group of girlfriends would each play a role on her wedding day, whether in the preparation, the speeches, or the execution of what would be the most magical wedding I have ever attended. But before all that romantic shit went down, I led this group of girls to Miami Beach for a decadent main bitch weekend.

The bachelorette party Instagram hashtag was #ChloesLastCock. It featured photos of us at the bar, on the beach, by the pool, eating, drinking, dancing, and raising toasts. There were photos of our cleavage, legs, ass cheeks, lips, and more. Also featured were graphic photos of the Haitian male stripper as he dry humped each and every one of us. (It's worth noting that Chloe was a professional dancer in her former life; she and a few of her dancer friends gave the stripper a real run for his money in the flexibility department, which made for great iPhone photos). After "Magnum" left, we bestowed upon Chloe a comprehensive collection of sex toys and devices, including Doc Johnson's Huge Realistic Black Cock, bubble gum-flavored lube, Mr. Moustachio, the Blow Job Bib, the Flash Brown Squirting Penis, The Just-In Beaver Blow Up Doll, and more—all of which are documented on Instagram, #ChloesLastCock.

While poolside, one of the girls took a photo of my cleavage, which looked particularly good in a push-up bikini top. She said, "that's hot, you should send that to your boyfriend." So I did. I thought Hector might appreciate the photo; it wasn't risqué or tasteless, it was just my way of saying, "Thinking of you."

No response.

A full day later, after trying really hard not to obsessively look at my phone during the time I was supposed to be focused on my girlfriends, I texted, "Hi Hector. Did you get my photo? One of the girls here took that photo and I thought you might like it, but no response? (sad-face emoji)."

A few hours after that: "Hi Madelyn. Thank you for the photo. I am sorry, I have just been really busy at work. I hope you're having fun."

Ouch.

Something was different. I instinctively knew something was different when I got no response to the photo. A girl just knows these things. Something was up.

I started to get really paranoid about Hector following me on Instagram, seeing all the crazy photos on #ChloesLastCock and jumping to inaccurate conclusions. Did I need to explain that no one had sex with the male dancer? Did I need to clarify that the sex toys were a joke? Did I need to spell out that we were just having some laughs and that the "big black cock" stuff was all just raunchy toilet humor? Did I need to assure him that one of my girlfriends took the photo I sent him and that I wasn't parading my B-cup cleavage around South Beach? If I needed to explain all that to the man I was with, then maybe there was something fundamentally wrong with the whole situation. After all, C-Lo and Lucky didn't even communicate the entire time we were on the trip and he was on his bachelor weekend. To me, that's true love.

I'd planned to bring up the odd feeling I'd had in Miami as soon as I got back and saw Hector. Something had shifted, though I couldn't put my finger on it, and it seemed important to clear the air and talk it out. But when we spent a day and night together, everything seemed fine again—so I decided not to ruin the moment and just enjoy his company. Maybe it was all in my imagination.

CHAPTER 22

THE WEDDING

Chloe's wedding was magical and she made the most stunning bride, as you would expect from the tall, athletic, stylish, creative, and beautiful woman that Chloe is. The wedding day was like a short film filled with romance, beauty, gorgeous scenery, love, music, and dancing. It took place at a mountain villa in Ojai, among breathtaking views, vineyards, and clean air. Close friends and family spent the days beforehand bike riding, hiking, sampling the vineyards, swimming, eating, and drinking together.

Hector joined me as planned. He'd suggested we visit his friends in Ventura prior to arriving in Ojai, but they were going to be out of town, so we went straight to Ojai. When we arrived at our hotel after the six-hour flight and two-hour drive, I was horny and ready to dive into bed and get it on—but Hector was antsy and unsettled. He paced around the room and kept finding excuses to do everything but get in bed. Let's get water. Let's unpack. Let's buy some wine. I'm hungry. Let's go for a swim.

What kind of role-reversal was this, where the woman is begging the man to stop futzing around and start fooling around? Am I that horny? Aren't guys usually the horny ones? I just didn't understand why love-making wasn't a priority, not just because we had taken a long trip, but we also hadn't seen each other prior to the flight for about a week.

I obliged all of Hector's whims and after a snack, a swim, and a Jacuzzi session with some wine, we finally had a quickie. It was satisfying, but this nagging feeling that something was different wouldn't quit. There was none of the usual passion. As a rule, Hector would moan something like, "Fuuuuuck Babyyyyyyy, Ahhhhhhh" at the moment of orgasm. This time, he was silent.

How could I possibly start raising issues while we were on this trip, at my best friend's wedding? I had bridesmaid-like responsibilities, a speech to give, and happiness to participate in. I was determined to keep things cool and not complain or raise any need for a "talk."

On the day of the wedding, the guests were to board shuttle buses at the hotel at 3:00 p.m. to take them up the steep and winding mountain road to the villa where the wedding would take place. I, however, being a main bitch, was required to be at the bridal suite in the villa at 11:00 a.m. to help Chloe get ready. The other three main bitches and I organized clothing, ironed ribbon-y things, steamed her dress, prepared snacks and pre-drinks, took selfies, and generally enjoyed our girlie time for the last hours of Chloe's bachelorette-ness. Hector stayed in the hotel room, saying that he had work to do for a few hours and would take the shuttle with the other guests.

When everyone started to arrive, Chloe and Luke were taking their "first look" photos. For the record, this is a term I had never heard before, but I put two and two together and assumed that I should be on hand to attack any dangling threads or flyaway hairs. As soon as I realized that the first-look moment was extremely personal and romantic, I made myself scarce and got busy primping and tending to my own beauty needs, which I'd neglected up until this point. When I saw the guests arriving, I slipped out of the bridal suite and gave Hector a quick pinch on the ass cheek, made sure he had some friends to hang out with, snuck him a drink of my champagne (the bar wasn't open yet), and told him I would be out in about twenty minutes. When I emerged after the photos, fully dolled up and camera-ready, I found Hector:

- Taking a selfie with the mountain view behind him;
- Not wearing the suit he brought, but something more casual;
- Wearing sporty canvas loafers, which I thought inappropriate for a formal affair;
- Complaining that the bar was not open yet.

Then he asked me to take a photo of him (alone) because his selfie didn't show enough of the mountains.

He never once complimented me or made any mention of how I looked, which was pretty lovely, if I do say so myself, in my appropriately short, asymmetrical-hemmed dress with tanned legs greased up like Beyoncé, but in a befitting-an-outdoor-California-wedding-in-90-degree-weather kind of way. I also had my hair and makeup done by HMU main bitch (HMU is a biz term for Hair Make Up), so you would have thought a compliment was in order. Or at least recognition from my boyfriend that I clean up nice.

I was consumed with nerves in preparation for my big speech, so once the bar opened, I started to imbibe. I didn't want to be too tipsy for my performance, though, so I was careful to pace myself. Hector, on the other hand, downed drink after drink after drink—it was probably a three-to-one ratio, his to mine. Being a 6'2" man, he had a much higher alcohol tolerance. But still.

The ceremony was lovely and touching. Luke and Chloe wrote their own vows, which were special and unique and the guests were all deeply moved by their exchange. They are clearly best friends who truly love each other. Girls were sniffling, guys were grabbing their girls' hands for a reassuring squeeze, parents were beaming, little girls were fantasizing. While I rustled through my small purse for a tissue to blot my tear, Hector sucked down his third vodka soda with a noisy slurp through a straw.

After more magical happenings that included an *a capella* original song sung by a friend (or an actual angel, I'm not sure which as I was tipsy at this point), a gospel choir that spontaneously emerged from the crowd after pretending to be guests, butterflies flitting around, a gentle breeze, warm sun, and dancing, we took our seats for dinner. Mine was at the head table, on the bride's right side. I was so honored to be sitting there. I was happy that on this momentous occasion, my man would be sitting to my right, encouraging me and supporting me as I prepared to deliver what I hoped would be a moving yet side-splittingly funny main bitch toast that would be captured on film and be a part of everyone's lives forever. And somehow Hector's being by my side for this moment would solidify our relationship, as we collect memories such as this and grow as a couple. So why didn't it feel like that?

My speech, the last of the night, the headliner, was a raging success. I told the story of how Chloe and I had met, which was over the phone on a business cold call, and it was girl-love immediately. She invited me to stay with her at her house in LA before we had even met in person, which was a testament to her warm and inviting nature, but also to our instant bond. I discussed the parallel nature of our lives, the ups and downs we seemed to experience in tandem that helped us to grow close as friends. I loaded the speech with lots of inside jokes and then segued into another language, which I dubbed "Chloe-ese" and spoke fluently, and everyone at the wedding understood. C-Lo had her own way of talking, of phrasing things, her own unique version of valley girl street slang.

Some excerpts of the Chloe-ese I spoke:

Girrrrrrrrrrrl. This wedding is dope. And Ojai is rad. C-Lo, you look gorge. Lucky, you so fine.

So dude. When C-Lo axed me to give a toast at her wedding, I was like, "Hey ma, do I have to keep it totally clean?" Because, well, I can be kinda foul sometimes. And she said "Nah, bish, keep it real." "F that," I said. "There's kids here, yo."

This wedding is totes off the chain. It has been super

rad to meet all you other hookers and dudes here.
We've had a blast over the last few days, riding our
bikes, hiking our asses off, and getting our drink on.
For realz.

Then I made a joke about how I'd be right back after I ran a quick seventeen miles and then would have preferred just some chicken broth for dinner instead of the amazing catered wedding food—a reference to C-Lo's constant marathon training and cleanse diets.

I got the laughs I had been looking for and the applause I had wanted and felt a giant sense of relief that the speech was successfully delivered. Now it was time to kick back, have a few carefree drinks, and dance. Hector wasn't really a dancer, so we just awkwardly floated around the dance floor for a bit. Then he went to the bar and made friends with another black guy. The two of them decided that it was the "blackest white wedding they'd ever been to," whatever that means. I stayed on the dance floor and danced with anyone who would join me.

Once we were back in the hotel room, exhausted and toasty from the long day, I had a hysterical laughing fit about something Hector said that was only marginally funny, then promptly passed out. Hector, however, stayed up for another three hours working on retouching a photo of ten of the world's most famous actors in a press shot at a charity dinner that was to run in the media the next morning. He had been working on the photo on and off all weekend long, but saved the majority of the work for the last minute. He could have skipped the previous days' bike ride or vineyard tour, but had decided to work on the photo while it wouldn't interfere with our fun time.

• • •

The next day, the bride and groom and all the other wedding guests were having a post-wedding-day pool party and barbeque, but, because I had dragged Hector across the country to a wedding where he knew no one, I thought it would be a considerate girlfriend thing to do to pass on the festivities and head down to LA where we had planned to connect with some of his friends from work. We took a beautiful scenic route drive to LA from Ojai and talked the entire way about how we'd love to return there. We'd visit his friends in Ventura whom we had missed on this trip, we'd visit certain vineyards we liked and explore ones we missed, and we'd take that long bike ride route again, but next time, just the two of us.

Hector seemed more relaxed and at ease now that the wedding was over. Maybe it was because he no longer had to interact with so many strangers. Or maybe it was because the retouching of Robert DeNiro, Leo DiCaprio, Al Pacino, and their famous friends was complete and delivered. We talked about how beautiful the wedding was, but agreed that it was more extravagant than either of us would ever want for our own wedding. I wouldn't go as far as to say that this conversation hinted at us getting married, but neither of us was saying "I don't want to ever get married," either. Sometimes guys say that. And sometimes I say that. But no one said it this time.

We checked into one of my favorite boutique hotels in LA but we never heard from Hector's friends. We had rushed out of Ojai, skipped out on my best friend's post-wedding pool party, and ended up spending the night in a much more expensive hotel in LA, for seemingly no reason.

I wasn't totally pissed off at this, though. We had enjoyed a lovely drive and some real quality time talking, which we are pretty good at. We ended up just having dinner in the hotel restaurant, for which I quickly threw on a dress, a light jacket, and a little bit of mascara and lip gloss. It was a minimal beauty effort for a casual quick dinner, but Hector complimented my outfit and told me I looked pretty. Yeah? Thanks a lot. Where was that compliment the day before, when I'd put forth all of that effort?

We were on a late flight home the next day, so we made the most of the time we had left in LA, and rode bikes through Santa Monica and Venice Beach, still talking about how much we liked California and making a long mental list of all the things we would do on our next trip out west. We took selfies together on the beach and on the bikes, and stopped for a moment to enjoy a long warm hug in the California sun. There had been a lot going on in my head about Hector's aloof behavior at the wedding, his subtle changes in behavior and lack of desire for sex. But after the reconnection I'd felt on the drive, that hug seemed to erase all of it. I felt safe again in his arms. Everyone has fears and issues at times, I told myself. Maybe I had been so consumed with pulling off my speech and my other main bitch duties that I was misinterpreting the signs. Maybe he had been stressing out about Robert DeNiro's skin tone. Maybe nothing was wrong at all.

Maybe.

It was late when we landed in New York, but instead of coming to stay at my apartment, as he had done after every other trip, Hector went back to his brother's place (where, at this point, he had been staying for eight months during his "roof renovation"). The reason he gave was that he had to get ready for work the next day.

CHAPTER 23

WRITTEN IN THE STARS

Every couple of years, I call on the higher spirits for help and guidance. What the fuck does that mean, you ask? I have an acquaintance, Denise, who is an astrological chart reader and spiritual, psychological consultant. She is terrific: accurate, insightful, funny, and delivers a tell-it-like-it-is-even-if-it's-not-what-you-want-to-hear New Yorker style kind of reading. The process is sort of like therapy but easier because you don't have to spend time telling your life story; she can fucking see it right there in the goddamn star chart.

The last time I saw her, Denise delivered a "MD-Is-An-Asshole" themed reading, just as he and I were breaking up. "Stay away from MD," she'd said (only she used his real name; I don't think she knew I referred to him as *Major Dick*. If she did, it might have swayed her reading just a little). "Say goodbye to him and move on. There are much better things on the horizon for you," she said quite emphatically, adding, "and sex. I see lots of hot sex." She also saw specific shifts in my job that turned out to be accurate, as well as some school-related issues with Imogen that were eerily on the money.

Besides being gifted, Denise was reliably good for a laugh in the darkest of moments and always delivered a reality check that knocked me off my ass into the present moment.

I had made the appointment much earlier in the year, mainly in order to examine my work situation but also to do a compatibility chart with Hector. Sometimes you just need the whiff of a higher power (real or fake) to validate your path in life and your feelings. The reading was scheduled for just after C-Lo's wedding, which turned out to be excellent timing, considering all the misgivings that had been rumbling around in my gut about Hector.

Denise had Hector's chart all ready when I arrived and she dove right in. She saw Hector constantly on the move, busy, traveling. "I see him on a bike," she said.

Hector rode his bike for hours on weekends.

She saw him having a lack of men in his life, which was uncanny because he had told me a deeply personal and very dramatic story about his father not being around much when he was young because, as it turns out, he had two wives. Suffice to say Hector's father was not so present, but Hector had always been very close to his mother (whom I still hadn't met). Also, there were seemingly no men in Hector's photography studio workplace; all of his colleagues and superiors he talked about were women. With her uncanny skill, Denise had zeroed in on the lack of manly presence in Hector's life.

She also picked up on the fact that Hector was the aloof and distant type. This made sense to me, but I had interpreted it as even-keeled and quiet and a bit shy. I had always felt that, while part of him was present with me, he was simultaneously off in his own thoughts. Denise saw the trouble he had staying still and was concerned that he was not staying still with me either. She didn't think there was another woman, but she saw that he was consumed with other parts of his life, especially work and more work. Also, work. She predicted that if Hector were to feel lack in any areas of his life, or if there were some emotional bump in the road, he would dive head first into work. But she did not see us breaking up. This stuck with me and gave me hope.

After we discussed my job, career path, and the idea for writing this book, as well as Louise's death and my new neighbors, Denise and I circled back around to the topic of Hector. She wondered, since I was questioning where we stood after we'd gotten off to such a good start, why I wouldn't flat-out confront him about my concerns. Why was I afraid to tell him that my needs were no longer being met? That I sensed some kind of change?

Well, we already know why I am such a pussy, don't we? Because I am deeply afraid of rejection. My modus operandi has always been, "If I just keep going at my usual pace, hold my breath and hold my tongue, wait for the bad stuff to pass, then everything will be OK. But if I speak up and make needy-girlfriend-type demands, my dude du jour will run for the hills in the blink of an eye."

Denise thought I was selling myself short (no shit) and encouraged me to move on if I wasn't getting what I needed from Hector, even though the cards didn't indicate that would be necessary. "Tell him that you're no longer feeling comfortable in the way the relationship is going and see how he reacts. And if you don't get the answer you want, go on one of those dating sites like Tinder. Don't sit around wondering. Get yourself out there, girl!"

I knew this was good advice. I didn't really need a $150 chart reading to tell me that I was selling myself short and needed to have a serious, honest talk with my boyfriend. But I guess I did need the $150 chart reading to kick my ass into gear to express myself.

CHAPTER 24

WHAT IS THIS…*"TINDER"*?

I like the written word. It is rarely misunderstood or misconstrued. It's clear and concise. You can take your time and deliberate over the perfect phrasing. You can't be misquoted or misinterpreted when you communicate in black and white. You can create a dramatic pause… with elipses. You can SCREAM!! Or you can state your case in a matter-of-fact manner. You can even emote ☺ as a last resort.

So, I chose the medium of the written word in which to communicate with Hector.

I wrote him a heartfelt, truthful, honest, and open email. I read and edited it over and over to make sure I'd said exactly what I wanted to say in perfectly clear, loving, non-confrontational, cooperative language. It went like this.

H,

It has been a little while since I have seen you. I didn't want much more time to pass before conveying to you some thoughts I've been having. Plus, you know how I like to communicate via the written word, so I thought this the best way to get my thoughts across.

I'm sorry to say that I have sensed a change in our relationship lately. I have noticed that our communication is not as strong and regular as it once was. It hurts my feelings that you don't reply to a text for a full day when you used to reply to me almost immediately. I miss the playfulness and sexiness in our texts and conversations that seem to be gone. You're more formal with me lately, and I feel very disconnected from you. And that really makes me sad.

I think you already know that I understand and value the need for space from each other on occasion. I never asked to be joined at the hip, and with both of our jobs and my responsibilities as a mother, our time apart is as precious as our time together. However, communication during the time that we are apart is also important to me. I thought we had found a perfect balance early on, but that seems to have changed.

I hope that it's my imagination and that maybe you're just distracted with your work. I know this promotion is something you've been working toward, so I'm very happy for you and excited at the new opportunities it will bring for you. I am looking forward to reconnecting with you and hopefully re-establishing our amazing connection. Soon.

Love,

M

I held my breath and hit SEND.

I stared at the computer. I stared at my phone. For five days.

• • •

The response I eventually got validated all of my fears.

> **Hi Madelyn,**
> **I was taken aback by your email. I am traveling for work, so I haven't had time to respond sooner. But I have thought a lot about what you're saying. I honestly thought I was going to have more time to spend with you this summer, but since I got promoted at work, I realize I won't have time to date.**
>
> **You deserve to be happy. Unfortunately with my new job, I will be too busy to give you what you want in a relationship. As much as I love you and miss you, I am sorry.**
>
> **We can meet for a drink and talk in person next week when I am back in town.**
> **Love,**
> **Hector**

There were so many things wrong with this email. Let's list them:

- It came five days after I sent mine.
- "Too busy for a relationship" is a cop out.
- We were doing more than "dating."

- He said he was "taken aback," making me feel as if I did something wrong.
- He suggested we meet and signed it with love, which he must have known would make a vulnerable and weak person feel like there was some kind of hope.

I managed to wait a day, then replied that I was sad to hear all this, but would love to get together and talk.

This is where shit got weird.

Big surprise, I waited another five days without a response from Hector, so I texted to follow up on the drink-and-talk suggestion. He replied right away and said Monday looked good (it was Friday), but that he would confirm later.

Monday came and went. I remembered what Denise said about moving on and getting myself out there. I didn't feel like going back to the same dating sites where no doubt the same losers would still be. I wasn't really in the mood to go through all of that again. I just didn't have it in me. But I also didn't want to sit around and pine for a guy who was clearly in the process of breaking my heart in a very immature and confusing way. As I was considering what my next move would be, I remembered Denise had mentioned Tinder. What exactly was it?

I quickly discovered that Tinder was an app originally created for horny people to find each other instantly, based on geographical as well as physical desirability (*read: hook-up app*). Very little information was required to join: a few photos, first name, age, and an optional short descriptive paragraph. Word on the street was that now everyone was using Tinder, and not just for a quick smash. In spite of itself, it had morphed into a veritable dating app.

Even though I was not positive that this was the right time for me to dive back into man-hunting, I loaded up the minimal requirements to make myself available on Tinder and went to work. Sometimes a little attention from a new dude is all it takes to make a dejected person feel better about herself. Luckily, Tinder was pretty easy and quick to navigate and, best of all, free. It took me a second to get used to the idea that my immediate YES or NOPE response to a particular guy would be final. A left swipe of the finger across my phone would banish that person from my feed, supposedly forever. A right swipe would be followed by notification of whether I was a match with this person—meaning that he gave me the right-swipe as well. Once matched, we could communicate via the app's messenger function and let the games begin.

OK, this could be fun, I thought. Or at least it could be an experiment to distract me from the doom and pain of heartbreak, sadness, confusion, and emptiness I was obviously about to experience. Again.

So I sat up straight, took a deep breath, and started swiping to see what might be out there. It was a bit hard to get used to the swiping action and I made a few errors. *Oops, I swiped right by mistake on that one. Phew, he wasn't a match.* I'd think I was scrolling to view more of a guy's photos, but was actually swiping NOPE or YES. *Swipe left...OH DAMN, he was cute!*

I wasn't sure why I was doing this in the middle of a workday, rather than concentrating on something important. I decided Tinder definitely had potential and planned to pick it up later, during some down time, but I really had to get back to work. I was just about to close the app and put the phone down when I swiped upon something that made me dry heave.

Hector.

Forty years old.

The photo I'd taken at Chloe's wedding, with the mountains of Ojai in the background.

This is where shit got weirder.

• • •

With trembling hands, I took a screen shot of Hector's Tinder page and texted it to him. "Nice photo," I typed through tears and serious dry mouth while my hands shook like a Parkinson's patient. I managed to cover my tracks, though, to retain my "innocence," by telling him that a girlfriend sent me that screen shot saying, "Isn't this your boyfriend?" Could happen.

I got a surprisingly immediate response.
   Hey Madelyn, Yeah, I joined Tinder recently, after I found out you were still seeing other guys.

Then he sent me a photo. It was a shot of what looked like an Apple iMessage conversation on a computer screen. It wasn't a screen shot of a text exchange on a phone. It wasn't an iMessage exchange on an iPad. It was undoubtedly a photo of a computer screen.

The iMessage conversation was between me and MixedBoy, aka Kevin, that took place just after he supplied me with my last fix; prior to my turning over a new leaf. The exchange was just slightly dirty, mostly "I had fun, did you?" kind of thing and "I keep thinking about the mirror." You know, the usual post-sex stuff.

I couldn't believe Hector had that conversation in his possession. Where on earth did it come from? How could he have acquired it? Did he snoop again? Did he somehow have remote access to my phone? Or to my computer? Did he install some kind of James Bond 007 spy device on my laptop so he could monitor the writings in the *Untitled* folder and somehow came across this iMessage exchange? I was so confused about how Hector acquired this image. But, more important, I felt the need to defend my innocence. Again!

I responded that the text in question was ancient history. I asked how he even got it. He told me that someone with an anonymous Instagram account Direct Messaged it to him in Instagram.

Can you believe that I actually believed that shit? My immediate reaction was that I desperately needed prove to Hector that this was another out-of-context piece of evidence against me and that I was nothing but faithful to him once we had our New Year's Eve talk. I couldn't fathom that he would be sneaky enough to actually violate my privacy like that. In my cloudy desperation moment, I didn't realize how absurd it would be for an anonymous Instagram account holder to have the motivation to seek out Hector and send him a conversation between me and MixedBoy; three people whose worlds do not at all collide. Was Hector implying that MixedBoy did it? Or perhaps a crazed jealous girlfriend Instagram stalker put together the connection between me and these two men? At the time, I didn't see this preposterous untruth right in front of me, mostly because I was still retching from swiping across my "boyfriend" on Tinder.

Next, I asked him why his response to supposedly receiving that photo was to join Tinder. Why wouldn't he instead confront me, give me the opportunity to explain, maybe give me the benefit of the doubt, like normal people who are in love with each other might do? Also, what about the "too busy to date" bullshit? He told me he had already been through all this before with me and he was done.

The story of how Hector acquired this photo haunted me for the next few weeks, as I pieced together bits of information like a detective. At the time, it seemed so complicated, convoluted and confusing, but now I realize it was just ridiculous. He just wanted out of the relationship, but couldn't muster up an upstanding way to make a clean break. I truly believed that I was finally being open and honest and monogamous in a good relationship (well, once we established that we were exclusive), and being accused of cheating hurt a lot. Wouldn't it have been more mature of him to just explain that he was no longer interested? As much as that would be hurtful and confusing, it wouldn't be steeped in deception, lies, and accusations.

I know how to lie so I am very perceptive when others are doing it. I was sure that Hector was lying about how he got the MixedBoy texts, and I was determined to figure it out. I may have been vulnerable, weak, and heartbroken, but I wasn't a gullible idiot. I was obsessed with uncovering the truth.

- I was able to figure out that there was no way a third party had access to that text conversation to screen-shot it and send it to Hector. Even Kevin himself or a crazed jealous girlfriend of his wouldn't have access to the conversation as it appeared. And how would anyone even know that Hector was my man? From monitoring our Instagram activity? Ridiculous.

- Furthermore, the iMessage exchange did not show names. Each person was represented by an avatar, and Kevin's was a photo that I took myself and assigned to him in my personal contacts. It wouldn't have been accessible from anywhere but one of my devices. My side of the conversation was represented by that generic human silhouette that comes with Apple devices. So this mysterious conversation between an Apple-generated generic human and my (beautiful) photo of Kevin could only have come from my computer.

- But I played dumb. I asked Hector how he even knew the exchange involved me. Assuming someone did indeed send it to him via Instagram, how could he identify the parties when there was only a generic human silhouette on one side of the conversation and a smiling handsome face on the other? Hector said he recognized the name Kevin because it always popped up on my phone.

- Liar. There were no names on the exchange.
- And besides, Kevin's name had not popped up on my phone since well before New Year's Eve. This was obviously some pre-New Year's Eve conversation jealous baggage that was just surfacing now in a very creative yet deceitful way.

There was only one way Hector could have obtained this photo and I'm sure you figured it out several paragraphs ago. Hector surely snooped through the iMessages on my password-free Mac and snapped a photo of the conversation. My best guess is that he did it while he was alone in the hotel room in Ojai before Chloe's wedding. I had been getting weird signals from him during the bachelorette party a month earlier, so I guess he had been looking for his way out. And what better way to extricate himself from our relationship blamelessly than to snoop and compile evidence against me? Maybe he'd been intending to look for more sordid tales in the *Untitled* folder but stumbled upon some juicy iMessages that served the purpose even better.

My heartfelt email plea to him made it all the easier to bail, simply by launching his "I'm too busy for you" bullshit. I had done the hard part for him by kindly pointing toward the exit. He was out. He wouldn't even have needed to accuse me of anything. But when I busted him on Tinder (not being fully certain that we *were* broken up, since he'd left the door open to "have a drink and talk"), he was armed and ready with the counterattack: incriminating evidence that screamed, "Back at you, bitch! It's all *your* fault. I didn't do anything wrong. I went on Tinder because *you* were cheating on me, and here is the evidence."

Hector was innocent. Even though he was busy on Tinder while he was supposedly "too busy to date." The whole thing was a giant mind-fuck.

● ● ●

In my haze of shock, disbelief, and desire to cling to Denise's words, "I don't see you breaking up," I didn't slam the door on Hector at that moment, even though I knew he was lying. I'd figured out that he'd snooped on my computer, lied about it, and then joined Tinder, but I *still* had a sliver of hope that this was all some kind of wild misunderstanding. I still believed, like I did after my husband left, that good relationships are not a dime a dozen, and that somehow he must have known that. Crazy, I know.

It's rare to connect with someone on multiple levels though, as Hector and I had, and you don't just throw that out the window as you would a fling. Believe me, I know how to identify a disposable fling and toss it out the window. I'm a pro at that. But, as illogical as it might sound now, I was clinging to the idea that the relationship was salvageable and we just needed some face-to-face, honest discussion about what had actually happened. Just as I had on New Year's Eve, I believed I *could* explain my side. And I would expect Hector to do the same. How could anyone flush a nice relationship like ours down the toilet so easily? I needed reasons. I wanted answers. I wanted logic.

I am aware that I annoy everyone in my life with my

need for logic and reason. It sometimes presents as the need to be right all the time. But in my mind, I don't need to be *right*. I just need to *understand*. Like a child...why? Why is that like that? Why is this like this? Why did you do it that way? Why can't we do it this way? Is there a reason for this being this way or is it arbitrary? Why don't meatballs bounce? Why is the goddamn sky blue? Why? I just want to *understand why*.

I don't know why my brain operates this way. Maybe it's because I'm a Libra? Some say I'm a control freak. But my behavior is not meant to be malicious; it's not egomaniacal and it's not controlling. Please, just explain everything so that I thoroughly understand and thus, moving forward, I will know how to act accordingly.

So, why did Hector lie? Why did he want to break up? What was the *real* reason? If I could understand it, maybe I could fix it. And if not, I would know that I tried and would accept the outcome. Maybe I could fix it for future relationships. Does this sound familiar? Jesus, woman, repeat patterns much?

I pestered Hector about meeting up for a drink and I was encouraged by his quick responses and willingness to schedule something soon. We eventually met at a place we regularly went to in my neighborhood. I thought this might be an attempt at reconciliation; otherwise why bother even meeting in person? I made sure I looked good and wore jeans that I knew he liked me (my ass) in. He showed up in shorts, a t-shirt, and flip-flops. That was my first signal that this was just an obligatory meet-up for him. My second signal was when he answered his phone while I was sharing my feelings. It was a quick conversation in Spanish, but he made no excuse and offered no apology for it.

We talked. I explained the texts. I brought my iPad to show him the dates on them, proving that they'd preceded our "exclusive" talk. It was like I was giving a goddamn PowerPoint presentation: *Here's how iMessages on iPhones look versus iMessages on iPads versus iMessages on computers. Whoever sent you that Instagram photo (*yes, I was still pretending I believed that*) must have hacked into my computer so I should now create a password, right? Look how there are no names here, so how did you know it was me? I haven't seen or spoken to Kevin in over six months, and the dates here prove it, see? So, do you think I should change my passwords on everything? Do you think my online security has been compromised?*

On and on I went, like a lawyer in court presenting evidence. I continued to ask him if I should change or add passwords on my computer, as if we were both victims in this horrific computer-hacking scam that almost ruined "us." I presented my case as if I needed his help, like I had back in November when he'd helped me set up the very computer that had now been tainted by an unknown hacker with nefarious intentions.

He was very quiet. Maybe he felt bad. Maybe he knew that I had busted him for snooping and was wondering why I was not flat-out accusing him. I had snooped on MD's American Airlines account, so maybe this was just evil karmic payback.

At one point, we were actually laughing and getting along like we used to and I started to tear up. I excused myself to go to the bathroom and when I returned, he had already paid the check. I was surprised by this, because earlier he had suggested that maybe we could grab a bite to eat. As we were leaving, he gave me a giant Hector-sized hug, which felt amazing and real. He told me that his mom had asked about me again. I called him "baby" when I hugged him and he called me "baby" back. I thought maybe we were going to be OK.

He texted me a few days later, when I was in LA for a video shoot:

It was njice to see you and talk, Madelyn. Let's get toger when you're back from your trip.

Njice? Toger? I don't want to seem like I'm overanalyzing things, but when you care about your communication with someone you don't let weird typos like *njice* and *toger* slip by, especially when you know how anal retentive that person is about spelling and grammar, which pretty much everyone who has ever met me knows. Didn't the Autocorrect work? It's a small thing, but it signaled carelessness, just as his shorts and flip-flops and Spanish phone call had. I pegged it as a perfunctory text and sentiment-free.

On the return flight from LA, I referred to Hector as "my boyfriend" while chatting with the person sitting next to me, and at that moment I realized that if he were indeed still my boyfriend, he would have known that I was on my way home. I would have let him know that the cabin doors were closed and I was shutting down. He would have said "have a safe trip," or "text me when you land." All those things that couples do. That we used to do.

I never heard from him again. He deleted our shared iCloud photo stream, which was loaded with photos from all our amazing trips, without warning. He unfollowed me on Instagram. This is how I learned for sure that my relationship of almost one year, with all its potential and wonderful possibilities and the hopes and dreams that went with it, was over.

CHAPTER 25

THERAPY COCK

There is a new trend that annoys me. Therapy dogs. Therapy dogs at the work place; therapy dogs at the grocery store; therapy dogs at the doctor's office; and most offensive, therapy dogs on the plane.

A therapy dog is not a service dog, like a seeing-eye dog. It's a dog trained to provide affection and comfort to people in hospitals, retirement homes, nursing homes, hospices, and to people with learning disabilities. This is legit. It's a valid occupation for a dog. The problem is, average everyday dog lovers are managing to get fake therapy dog licenses for their precious stupid pets, citing the need for comfort in average everyday situations. It's like dog carte blanche. To me, it's the same as stoners getting medical marijuana licenses. I mean...come on. You don't *really* need that.

I am not a dog lover. Sorry. Jesus, calm down. I'm not a dog hater either, but I think pets have their place and that place is at home or in a yard, drooling and shedding on the people who love them. Anyway, I actually might be allergic to dogs, so give me a break. I am allergic to dogs in the same way I am allergic to shellfish. I had a strong reaction as a kid, but it has been so many years since I actually ate shellfish, I am not sure if I am still allergic. Similarly, I avoid petting dogs in case I break out into some kind of hideous rash. I might be allergic. I might not. So when there is a dog sitting in the lap of the woman next to me on a plane, I become uneasy.

"Excuse me, I'm sorry, but is your dog going to be in your lap the whole flight? I'm allergic to dogs and this is a long flight for him to be so close to me."

"Oh, why yes he is," replied the tall, thin, bleached blonde, collagen-lipped, high-heel-wearing, aging ex-model, in a baby voice. She seemed to be addressing her answer more to the dog than to me.

When I politely asked the flight attendant to move the dog and his owner because of my allergy, you'd have thought that I asked her to euthanize it. The flight attendant assured me that the dog would have to be on the floor for the flight, and not in the woman's lap, hence her extra-leg-room seat.

"Well, even on the floor, the dog is still very close to me," I said, trying to sound reasonable. "And also," I smiled in the direction of the nice model lady, "she's told me she prefers to keep the dog in her lap and not on the floor. So maybe there is another seat somewhere for the two of them?"

The entire plane was up in arms.

"I love dogs! I'll sit there."

"I think it's great that we have a dog on our flight!"

"Leave the dog alone! What an asshole!"

"My dog looks just like that! I'll sit there!"

"Hello! Can we please close the cabin door? Who gives a shit about a dog?"

"I'm allergic too, get that dog off this plane!" (*A voice of reason among the angry mob*).

"C'mon lady, you got some nerve. Let someone else sit there."

Let it be known that I was in 7A, the front-row bulkhead window seat just behind first class, with legroom for days. Thanks, but I'd rather blow my nose and scratch my hives for six hours than give you this prime seat and sit in your crap middle one.

The flight attendant had left the scene during all this badgering, to call on the gate manager for help. At his simple suggestion, I traded window seats with a dog lover in 7F, which was identical to 7A. The entire plane applauded as I got up to move.

If said dog-lover in 7F had volunteered to move twenty minutes earlier, she'd have spared everyone the drama. And, for the record, I still think the whole thing was grossly unfair. Why couldn't Blondie and Fido have traded middle seats? Why was I the one who had to move? Regardless, I settled into my new seat wearing a Scarlet H for (dog) Hater.

My new seat neighbor was an off-duty flight attendant who shook her head in sympathy. "New rules. Ridiculous. Are you OK?"

I got teary and wanted to hug her. "Thank you, I'm fine."

"Write a letter," she advised. "I would do it too, but," she pointed to her airline employee badge, "I can't."

• • •

I would like some new rules, too. When I am feeling sad or lonely, I like to have sex. It makes me feel better about myself and it's calming and relaxing. I need therapy cock. And I would like a therapy cock license that would permit me to travel with a hot trainer on my lap. He wouldn't pee or poop, drool or shed. He would only require a little water. He wouldn't bark or grunt or growl at anyone. No one would be allergic to him. When I was feeling nervous during takeoff, I could stroke his cock for comfort. He'd nuzzle up against me and gently kiss my ear and I'd feel safe and loved. I could squeeze his cock if there was turbulence during final descent. Therapy cock would provide me the same comfort, affection, and sense of calm that the therapy dog is meant to provide for others.

CHAPTER 26

BARF, CRY, HATE

After I finally accepted the fact that Hector was gone, I still didn't accept the fact that Hector was gone. I'd given it a tonnage of thought, but I still never really figured out quite what happened. It's not just me that does this, it's a girl thing, isn't it? We *need* to know *why*. You could come up with a hundred possible reasons (and by now, you know I'm going to subject you to a list), but none of them might be true or all of them might be true. Or maybe some are true and some aren't. Regardless, you know you'll wake up one day and realize that none of it even mattered because he was *just gone*. But until that day, you analyze and replay everything that had happened, trying to find a logical and sound reason for his exit so that you might avoid a similar situation in the future. After all, we want to better ourselves for when the next supposed soul mate shows up, so we won't fuck it up again…assuming we fucked it up in the first place.

So why does a guy with whom you have enjoyed a great ten-month relationship suddenly disappear like a ghost? Here is an assortment of possibilities:

- He was scared of commitment.

- He had a wife and kids at the home you never saw.
- He decided to prioritize work and honestly just didn't want to be in a steady relationship.
- He met someone else who was younger, prettier, and skinnier.
- He snooped through your diary and realized that you'd slept with enough men before him to officially make you a slut.
- You farted that one time.
- He decided he wants kids and you're too old.
- You're too old.
- He saw photos online from your friend's bachelorette party and he was disgusted by your crass and foul behavior (even though you didn't really do anything wrong, you were just being silly).
- You earn more money than he does and that fucks with his masculinity.
- You earn the same amount of money that he does and that fucks with his masculinity.
- You earn less money than he does and that rules you out as his sugar mamma.
- Your sense of humor was endearing at first but now you're not funny anymore.
- Turns out he just wasn't that into you after all.
- He snooped through your diary on your computer because he knew it had no password and learned that you slept with a super hot guy about two months after you started seeing each other, even though deep down he knew that you had not yet had the "we are exclusive" conversation, but he thought it was understood and he was hurt by this

and just never could get over it, plus who's to say that it won't happen again because you still run into this guy and his name appears on your phone sometimes, even though it's just a friendly "hello" text, but also you're constantly surrounded by all those other hot guys at the gym and in your work environment so you'll probably do it again after you get bored of sex with him so he'll just break up with you now to avoid all that hurt that's inevitable, like how his dad cheated on his mom, because he does really love you but he'd rather be the breaker instead of the breakee, so fuck it.

I spent days, weeks, and months thinking about ways to reach out to Hector to explain and convince him to get back together because I thought the relationship, despite all its faults, was worth saving. I composed draft emails that said things like, "We should talk about whatever the issues are because we had such a great time. A connection like that doesn't come along every day and once we had the 'exclusive' conversation, I was honestly solid with you, so we should try to talk and work things out..."

Zzzzzzzzzzzzzzz. Oh, sorry, I dozed off again because I'm so bored of this shit.

I was guilty of constantly scheming to find ways to reach out to Hector. I could ask him what the name of that restaurant was. I could say that I finally saw that movie, he should really see it. I could tell him that I found that sweatshirt he had been looking for. I could tell him that I saw his good friend Eduardo on Tinder and...but didn't

Eduardo have a girlfriend?*

It was a very scary proposition, but I knew that communicating with Hector would be a fruitful exercise. If he were open to communication, maybe I could get some answers. Maybe, just maybe, a reconciliation would be possible. If he ignored me, then I could finally officially close the door and move on. It was a step that I needed to take because even though deep down I knew it was over, I needed to confirm it. Again. One last time. Girls do this. Is it *really* over? Yes, bitch, it's really over. But if you need to have it spelled out in bright red large blinking neon lights, then go right ahead and send your email.

Riding a big Mandingo trainer cock after a good workout leaves a girl feeling carefree and gives her exactly the right amount of self-confidence to email her ex-boyfriend. So, after my morning therapy cock, I was feeling particularly saucy and bold. I emailed Hector to say Happy Birthday. Don't think that I hadn't had my eye on the calendar for about three and a half weeks, waiting for that date to arrive. It was the perfect excuse to reach out to him with the hope that he would see how nice I am to remember his birthday, recall that we were supposed to be in Trinidad with his family at this very time, get a bit sentimental, and invite me to have a reconciliatory beverage.

Crickets.

• • •

Here's a tip. When you're trying to pull your shit together after a breakup, don't work from home. If you work from home, there is virtually nothing stopping you from

YouTube'ing a sad song, busting out into a good five-minute cry, and then hitting the kitchen cabinet for a cookie (OK, seven cookies) or some chips (many, many chips), which is the only thing you'll eat all day. You can also just get up from your desk and move over to the couch to play Candy Crush for an hour because it helps you to zone out and numb your thoughts. You can take a nap after.

Instead, go out and get yourself one of those shared office spaces that are all the rage now where you're constantly surrounded by other humans, some of whom might even be dateable, but all of whom are up in your grill all day preventing you from descending into a fit of sadness where you barf, cry, and hate—not necessarily in that order. But when you're around people who are having lunch, you smell food and get hungry. You wander over to the common kitchen where you interact with someone and maybe even laugh. And the next day you meet someone in the hallway who makes your loins get all fired up and you remember that you're capable of liking a guy again.

* My theory is that the two of them, Hector and Eduardo, were complaining to each other about their women, and Eduardo suggested they ditch them and move on. Fuck those bitches and let's go on Tinder together. Eduardo was a real asshole from what I knew about him (three different baby mamas, rude, misogynistic, and neglectful of child support payments, you know the type). He was also Hector's world travel partner before I showed up and he was undoubtedly jealous. I believe that some of Hector's odd behavior was influenced and/or coached by that prick.

CHAPTER 27

YOU'RE NEVER GHANA BELIEVE THIS

Email to Chloe:
> I accidentally dated a 21-year-old.

Email response from Chloe:
> I'm not surprised. Do I dare ask for details?

Ugh, it's not even fun anymore. I can't even get a rise out of Chloe with a ridiculous email like that. What is this world coming to? I mean, it's not even that controversial or exciting, but the point is that the motherfucker was twenty-one. Twenty. One.

Email to Chloe with unsolicited details:
> Did I tell you about my new office space? I rented an office in a shared workspace called U-Work. It's no corner suite, but it has three desks and lots of space so that I can take meetings and comfortably work from somewhere other than my dining room. It's been great for getting me out of the house and my apartment is much less

cluttered with papers and shit everywhere.

The very first day I moved into the space, literally as I was walking down the hall with the key to my new office in my hand, a super-cute young black guy popped out of his office and said "Hi!!"

I looked upward and whispered, "Thank you" to the universe.

He looks a lot like HMN and I felt instantly connected to him. We really hit it off. By the end of the day we had exchanged numbers and he was texting me, "So glad you're my office neighbor" and "See you tomorrow."

He is an ex-professional soccer player from Ghana and he and his ex-teammate from Brazil are using their soccer money to start an app development business. They are both beyond smart and sweet and well-mannered...but young. I wasn't quite sure how young, but one day I was chatting with the Brazilian and he mentioned something about being 24 years old. I thought (hoped) that HOGG (Hot Office Ghana Guy) was at least a little older. I never bothered to ask because it just didn't matter. I was just happy to have a few interesting and handsome individuals to interact with on a daily basis.

Email response from Chloe:
Whatever works, freak.

Our U-Work office space had just been built, so we were among the first ones to occupy the mostly vacant floor. HOGG and I behaved like school kids, getting lunch together and holding hands, sneaking off to the empty common areas and stealing kisses, texting each other "hi" from across the hall. Then we stepped it up a notch by sharing a printer and I gave him the spare key to my office so that he could use my space to work alone or take a meeting when I wasn't there. This was very generous of me, I know. I liked HOGG a lot.

I recognized that one day I'd snap out of this fantasy into reality, but for now, it was exactly what I needed to get my mind off of Hector and help me to transition back to my normal, fun-loving self.

After a few months, HOGG's app company started to pick up steam. They were working around the clock to attract clients and had several proposals in the works. HOGG started to travel often. They recruited more young handsome soccer players. They grew out of their office across the hall from me and moved to the other side of the floor, to a bigger space. I saw him less and less during the day, which was probably a good thing because our proximity was starting to become a distraction for both of us. We had to make more of an effort to connect. The floor was starting to fill up, so our kitchen and common areas were no longer our private playgrounds where we could kiss and touch. We had lost our groove.

I arrived at my office one morning to find some of his papers and documents on my desk. There was a receipt, a travel itinerary, and a copy of his passport in a messy pile. I didn't actually snoop, as all of this was openly facing me. Without even having to touch the papers (OK, I barely shifted them), I saw his passport date of birth was Christmas Day, 1993.

I'd accidentally dated a twenty-one-year-old. I didn't mean to.

And you know what else is weird? MD's birthday was also Christmas Day. Maybe I should just date Jesus, if he ever actually comes back.

One day, HOGG walked in to my office with a look on his face. I wasn't sure what the look meant, but I knew it wasn't good. In that nanosecond when the cerebellum interprets information sent to the brain by the eyes, a million thoughts flew through my head:

- He figured out how old I am.
- He is being deported.
- He needs money.
- He is seeing someone his own age.
- He found out I was seeing someone else. (Wait. Was I? I couldn't remember at that moment.)
- He is moving his office again.

HOGG sat down, touched my hand, looked me deep into my eyes and told me they were moving their app business to San Francisco, where it obviously belonged. We professed our love for each other at that moment and vowed to stay in touch. I think we both needed each other at the time we met to help us plant our respective feet back on the ground. We had each been swaying in the breeze and needed grounding, which we did for each other during our few months together. After HOGG, I could begin to understand why teachers claimed to fall in love with their students. Eww, I know it's a little sick, I am well aware, but I *can* sort of relate. And, as cliché as it may sound, I can't say I was in love with HOGG, but I can definitely say that I loved him. We cared for each other and I hope we can always stay friends. It is also worth noting that at a worldly and wise twenty-one years old, HOGG had a much more mature way of handling himself than any of my last 34,000 boyfriends who were within a decade of my age. And for the record, HOGG and I never actually had sex.

• • •

My office space is now teeming with young millennial hipsters (*read: fucking assholes*). All the offices are filled, the kitchen is jammed with people lunching, talking, laughing like a goddamn university cafeteria. The ladies room is no longer mine alone. The elevators take forever and are packed. The walk down the hallway is no longer exciting and I don't get butterflies at work anymore. No one else at U-Work has even spoken to me, let alone caught my eye, since HOGG left. I've been getting a lot more work done, though.

HOGG was a gift from the universe at a time I really needed it.

CHAPTER 28

DEAR MADELYN

Dear Madelyn,

Hope you are well. I know that I am not your favorite person right now, but I hope you'll take the time to at least read my email, lol.

I have done a lot of thinking about us and about what happened. I am sure you know, I was not completely honest with you. I always knew you had other men in your life and I was never comfortable with that, even if they were only friends or ex-lovers or whatever. I looked on your computer while you were at your friend's wedding just to see if there was any more suspicious behavior. The temptation was too great once you were out of the hotel room for such a long period of time. I guess I always just assumed you were still seeing other men and that you would end up wanting to be with one of them instead of me. I felt threatened.

I am sorry for lying about it. I am more sorry for the way I handled the whole thing. I am embarrassed, to say the least, and I don't know how you could ever forgive me. I realize now that you are the love of my life and that I was so afraid of losing you to another guy that I created the scenario in my head. I guess it was my way of controlling the situation so that I didn't get hurt. And in that process, I know that I hurt you.

I hope you will forgive me some day. I hope even more that I might have another chance with you, and for us. I know that we can be happy together for a long time, like you said, but it would require me to open up and let go of fears that I didn't even know I had. I would be willing to try, if you could ever find it in your heart to forgive me.

If not, I totally understand, and I will live with the mistake that I made and the guilt that I feel for lying and hurting you. I will always love you, Madelyn. I think you know that.

Love,
Hector

• • •

I actually never received that letter. It was something I concocted in my head because I thought I *should* receive it. Maybe by typing it out I could manifest its reality. I still needed answers badly for why Hector just disappeared, with no real chance for closure. I clung to the concept that he might regret what happened so desperately that I wrote this letter to myself, hoping that I would create some version of it in real life.

I never did hear from Hector again. Sometimes I walk by places we used to go to and get all choked up. Every time I am in the neighborhood of his office, I keep my head down for fear of seeing him. Thank God I don't live anywhere near where he lives. Of course, I don't even know where that is. I still feel a little suspicious about that, but I guess it doesn't matter at this point. Actually, it's the Oxford English Dictionary definition of "doesn't matter at this point."

I stayed annoyingly sad about it. I was thoroughly irritated with myself over the sadness and obsessive contemplation this breakup brought. Why couldn't I shake these feelings? We were together for less than a year! But we'd packed a solid relationship and five exciting trips into that short amount of time, so it felt like longer. Because I had harbored hopes for the future with Hector, the breakup hurt way more than my breakup with MD, and that excuse for a relationship had lasted five years. I'm exasperated by my getting teary as I type, so I'd better change the subject to something a little more upbeat—like hot sex.

CHAPTER 29

BBC

Just for the record, I was on the BBC* tip way early. Nowadays it appears that many white girls are discovering the joys and pleasures of the BBC, but having grown up in Philadelphia—which they don't call "the City Of Brotherly Love" for nothing—I was exposed to young BBC very early.

I'm not sure I can explain why I became attracted to men of color. As a kid, I don't even think I knew the difference. Up to a certain point, kids don't see race. It's only as we become adults and are subjected to the biases manufactured by society that we develop boundaries and racism. For me, favoring the BBC was never an exclusive thing. After all, my ex-husband is one of the whitest people you'd ever meet, almost translucent, having been born and raised in North Dakota. I've bounced back and forth between black, white, and "other" my whole life, with no specific reasons for why I was physically attracted to one person over another. But...what can I say? I find something very masculine about black guys that white guys don't possess. A toughness. A strapping, manly quality that turns me the fuck on.

My first serious crush was on a feisty, basketball-playing fellow fifth grader, Lionel Washington. He may have liked me too, in a fifth grade kind of way, because he teased me by calling me "Nubs," a reference to my nipples, which had developed way before the breasts they were attached to. His other nickname for me was "Shaggy Dawg," thanks to my long, unkempt, frizzy brown hair. I preferred Shaggy Dog to Nubs, but I secretly enjoyed both pet names because they meant that Lionel Washington was paying attention to me.

My next crush was on a light-skinned, very bright, quiet, sweet boy with a giant, prize-winning Afro named Stanley White. I didn't interact much with Stanley White except for the one time when I couldn't stand it anymore and planted an innocent kiss on the cheek of the stunned and very shy boy at fifth-grade graduation.

I don't remember ever seeing Stanley again after that, but I did stay friends with Lionel until eighth grade. He was hilariously funny as well as some kind of genius. He had a horrible work ethic, acted out in class, yet aced every test and got straight A's. Lionel was one of those kids who was finished with the test about an hour before everyone else and spent the rest of the time making jokes and singing and generally disrupting things while everyone else was trying to concentrate. I still remember Miss Shuster's "*SSSSSHHHH.* Lionel!"(pronounced with the accent heavily on the 'NEL, as in Li-o-NEL). I think she would have ridden his ass a little harder if he hadn't always aced every damn test.

I tried to find Lionel on Facebook recently, thinking it would be kind of fairy-tale-like if we reconnected after all these years and got married or something. But the only Lionel Washington I found in the Philadelphia area is currently a preacher. I can only hope that's not my Lionel.

The point is, while I have loved the BBC since before it was some kind of trendy thing, now my competition for it is much stiffer (pun intended). Every white, Asian, Spanish, and whatever chick is now hot for the BBC, as if the tall, handsome, fit black guy the BBC is attached to is some kind of in vogue fashion accessory. I can't wait until this trend is over because I was first.

*BBC = Big Black Cock

CHAPTER 30
GETTING INTO MY DRAWERS

I have a big black dick. It's about eight inches long and an inch-and-a-half wide. I keep it in my nightstand drawer. I also have a white dick about the same size, but it's a little longer (ironically), and skinnier. The white dick is actually my friend Matthew's dick. He was in a band that I worked with at one of my label jobs and we became very close friends. We never "dated" (that's the polite way to say we never fucked), but we talked about sex all the time. It was great getting a guy's perspective on things, and in turn, he wanted the female perspective. So, while he was on tour in Detroit, he went to a porn store and bought a penis casting kit and Fed Ex'ed his dick to me at work. He asked me to "use" it and report back.

Matthew's dick had a little curve to it. He wanted my opinion on that curve, as he gets mixed reviews. Some girls think it hurts and some girls tell him it hits just right and is extremely pleasurable. Personally, I enjoyed Matthew's dick tremendously. I liked it better than the big black dick because Matthew's was slightly skinnier and the black dick was a tad too fat. But for the sake of accurate reporting, I wished that Matthew hadn't bought the penis casting kit with the vibrating option. The vibration was hard to resist, so I don't think I really gave him a fair assessment.

The big black dick and Matthew's dick are just for me. I have other toys for joint use as well as some lube and assorted condoms in another drawer in the same nightstand. The regulars know where to reach when it's time to wrap up, or lube up, or whatever.

One day I came home to Imogen doing her homework in her room (do they still call these latchkey kids?), as usual. I went into my room to change into yoga pants and a tank top, as usual. I sat down on the bed to peel off my jeans, as usual. Imogen came in my room to do a somersault on my bed, her usual form of greeting, and then bounced off to her room. For the record, this is a normal occurrence. Sometimes she somersaults to say hello, sometimes she does it to say goodnight and sometimes she spontaneously bounds into my room to somersault for no reason. But it is always perfectly executed and it always messes up my covers and pillows. I act annoyed, she laughs, and just like that, we've shared a moment.

But this time I noticed something unusual post-somersault. A piece of the comforter on my bed was stuck in the nightstand dick drawer, as if the drawer had been opened and then closed on the corner of the comforter. I tugged at the comforter and it came loose, causing the drawer to open just a hair. I wondered how that could have happened. The cleaning lady had come the day before but I had slept in my bed since then. Surely I would have noticed the corner of the comforter stuck in the nightstand when I got in bed, or it would have come loose at that point.

Suddenly my face became hot and flushed. A bead of sweat dripped down my back and the hair on my neck became moist with sweat. I was having a hot flash, yes. But what spurred it on was the thought that Imogen had been snooping in my room when she was home alone and opened that drawer. There was no other logical explanation for the corner of the comforter being stuck in my dirty-sex drawer.

"Imogen?"

No answer.

Louder, "Imogen?!"

Nothing.

"IMOGEN!!!" borderline screaming.

"WHAT???"

"Come back in here, please?"

Imogen took her headphones off, apologized for not hearing me, and dutifully reported to my room.

I pointed, "The corner of my comforter was stuck in the nightstand over there. That's weird, right? How do you think that could have happened?"

"I don't know, that IS weird. Maybe it got stuck when I did the somersault?" There was a strange tone to her voice. It was really friendly and upbeat. Normally, she would have shrugged and walked away without an intelligible word or with an attitude-laden "Uh-unnoh" (*translation:* I don't know.).

"I don't think so." I persisted, "I don't see how that could happen from your doing one somersault."

"Weird, yeah. That's weird. OK, well, I'm going back to my homework now."

I was super suspicious. But I didn't want to accuse

her of anything and embarrass us both. What if she was innocent?

But what if she wasn't? Was I so naïve and trusting to think that she would never snoop in my room? She had lived in the same apartment her whole life; what mysteries could she have been looking for? We leave the door open when we pee, we talk about tampons versus pads and we openly fart in front of each other. It had never occurred to me to hide my sex accouterments more carefully than I had. The nightstand is on the far side of the bed in a corner. It isn't easy to access unless you're in the bed. What could have prompted her to climb over the bed to look in those drawers? Why? What did she think I might be hiding?

Don't answer that.

The next day after Imogen left for school, I frantically cleared out both drawers. I was kind of sad to stash Matthew way back in the deep dark depths of my closet. I liked him better in the deep dark depths of me. I carefully wrapped him up in the red bandana that he'd come in (by *come* I mean *arrived*) and told him, "Don't worry, my friend, I won't forget you're back here. And you won't be lonely, Tyrone will keep you company." I put the condoms and lube in a new hiding place as well, thoroughly annoyed because in the new location they wouldn't be nearly as handy whilst in the heat of the moment as they were before. I wanted to write two giant notes and slip them into each empty drawer, one saying "HELLO IMOGEN!" and the other, "GO DO YOUR HOMEWORK!" But I decided against it.

Then I strategically placed the comforter and the pillows in a very specific spot that would require moving them to open the drawer. I also positioned a piece of tissue paper just inside the drawer so that it would fall in if the drawer were opened. What I really wanted to do was rig up one of those trip wires that would signal to me that someone had crossed the line, but I didn't have this kind of technology. The bedding and the tissue were going to have to be enough.

I went off to work feeling smug because I am slicker than my kid.

That afternoon, I got Imogen's usual daily text, asking, "What time will you be home?" I always answered immediately and truthfully because I figured she just wanted to know when her mommy was coming home. It had never before occurred to me that there might be secret snooping things going on while I wasn't there. This day, I didn't answer the question right away and she asked me again, "What time are you coming home?"

"I'll be home in about two hours, or maybe sooner," I responded, but the truth was, I was on my way home and would be home within fifteen minutes.

When I walked in the door, I half expected her to be scrambling to exit out of my room. Instead, she was sitting on the couch having a snack, as cool as could be. "That was a fast two hours," her smart ass said.

I bee-lined into my room. I didn't even care if she saw me head over to the scene of the alleged crime. Alas, the evidence was inconclusive. I *thought* the comforter and pillow were in a *slightly* different position, but I couldn't be sure. The tissue was almost where I had put it, but it might have moved a little, though. Damn, I should have taken a photo of everything so there would be no shadow of a doubt. But I did think the comforter was slightly askew. This could have been a result of a somersault, although these were unlikely to happen without an audience. I couldn't be sure, so I didn't accuse her of anything.

The next day, I upped my sleuthing game. I took a photo of the exact positioning of the pillows. When I returned home and checked the scene, everything was exactly as I had left it. Ditto, the next day. I wondered if she had in fact snooped again that first day and, seeing that the drawers were now empty, had known that she was busted. There was nothing left to snoop for so there had been no further attempts since then.

How mortifying. But, the kid should not have snooped. If she did. But, what kid doesn't snoop? In retrospect, I realize that I should have better hidden Matthew and Tyrone (the black dick isn't really called Tyrone, I just named it earlier in this chapter, so I guess the name will stick). I remember snooping in my big sister's room when I was a little younger than Imogen. I found a box of tampons in her dresser drawer and asked my mother what *tampons* were. She asked me why I was asking. Half hoping to get my big sister in trouble, I said, "Donna has them in her room."

"So go ask Donna," she told me.

When I asked Donna, she said, "Go ask Mom."

I can't remember how I learned what tampons were, but I'm sure that neither of those bitches told me. I probably went back to take another look and read the instructions in the box. I had three big sisters and a mother; you'd think one of them would have told me what the fuck tampons were, at least, if not lay the facts of life and womanhood on me at some point. Instead I had to learn it all from snooping.

I wonder what Imogen learned from her alleged snooping...that she didn't already know.

CHAPTER 31
CHLOE NON-UPDATE

Email from Chloe:
 Subject: Cock
 Now that I have your attention, give me a fucking update.

Email to Chloe:
 Re: Cock
 Yup, cock always gets my attention.
  The fucking update is that in one of your old emails you said, "If everything falls apart with MrHH, you can go back to being a total slut." Well, guess what?!

After I updated her on the finality of the Hector situation, Chloe suggested that I wasn't the only one who noticed he was behaving a little weirdly at the wedding. (How horrible, I thought, that my best friend's memories of her own wedding are tainted with all that shit going on behind the scenes!) I admitted to her that I had probably been ignoring some ominous signs prior to the wedding, but I didn't feel the need to rehash all that shit. We just decided to Photoshop him out of the wedding photos wherever we could. Oh, the irony.

Email to Chloe:

It's time to move on, sister. And we know what that means! There is a hole in my heart. I shall fill it with cock until I am numb.

Email from Chloe:

I totally understand the desire for steady cock. I had fun for a while being a ho too, but after a while it's just a lot of work for so little pay-off. Maybe just have some you time right now and work on your writing. That was my favorite shit to do when I was heartbroken. Try just doing you, 24/7. Work out, go on little weekend trips, do new things in the city you haven't done before with your girl, all that good shit. Annnnnyway, loves you! C-Lo

This simple, yet powerful advice is pretty wise. Just do me. It's a good idea in theory. Theoretically, yes, I wanted to do me. However, doing me, for me, is doing *it.* So I had Soul Fucker handle the job of doing me as much as possible during this recovery time frame. I realize this is contradictory (yes, I said contra-DICK-tory) to the wise advice of C-Lo and to my gut instinct about how to heal. But I had rediscovered premium drug-like pleasures and escapism with Soul Fucker.

What does happiness smell like? It's a fact that the sense of smell is closely linked with memory, more so than any of our other senses. A smell can spontaneously evoke particular memories, acting as a trigger in recalling an event or experience or a person, for better or worse. No doubt you've experienced this yourself. Marcel Proust, in *Remembrance of Things Past*, very poetically wrote that a whiff and a bite of a madeleine cookie (yes, a bite of delicious *me*) made him vividly recall childhood memories of his aunt giving him the same before going to church on Sundays, and all the sentiments that went with that.

For me as a kid, happiness smelled like the legendary Termini Brothers Italian bakery in South Philly. The scent of freshly baked cannoli, pastries, and cakes filled the shop so strongly that the smell would linger in my hair long after I left. A visit to Termini Brothers with my dad meant not only was I in for a special treat, but it must have been a special occasion or holiday at my family home. In general, this meant there would be no household tension, no stress around my having to do homework or practice the piano or any other parental pressure on me to excel in some superior way.

In college, happiness smelled like weed. I was never one to actually smoke myself, but weed had replaced cannoli in the olfactory representation of a stress-free environment. If I smelled weed, it meant there was no pressure to accomplish something important at that very moment, because wherever I was, we were chilling.

As a wife and new mother, happiness smelled like sautéed garlic. It meant we were home, cooking. In my kitchen. As a family. *My* family.

Now, happiness smells like Versace Eros. Soul Fucker's cologne. It lingers on my skin and in my hair, making me want to delay showering after an encounter as long as possible. That smell...of temporary, fleeting, impermanent happiness. But what other kind of happiness is there? Damned if I know.

I knew I could not live forever in this sort of sex-as-drug haze, numb to everything. It was not reality. It was more like hypocrisy. A form of self-abuse. I am not a nymphomaniac, but I am an attention addict. To know that this beautiful (though unavailable) man that I had put on a pedestal of sorts desired me and wanted me as much as he wanted to please me was thrilling. I was in a haze of attraction and the hottest sex imaginable, like an animal running on pure carnal instinct. There was no thought or reasoning behind my actions, no fear of repercussions, no guilt, and no judgment. There was no choice, almost, and there was also no winning and I knew it. Whatever. The whole thing was impossible to resist, so neither of us tried to.

One afternoon in my apartment, before re-entry into the real world but after re-entry into me, Soul Fucker and I shared a few drinks. We chatted, laughed, talked, shared more than we ever had before. For a second, I caught myself enjoying his company tremendously. Not only was he just the finest man I have ever laid eyes on, but he was well-educated, very funny, charming, witty, interesting, deep—all the things you want in your man. As an added bonus, he cooked us up a delicious late lunch in my kitchen, and topped off the day by fixing a loose kitchen cabinet door. Whoa. A giant alarm buzzer sounded and a flashing red police light lit up my bedroom. *CLANG CLANG CLANG!!!!* ***WARNING! DANGER AHEAD! FEELINGS DEVELOPING! DANGER! DANGER!***

• • •

The flashing lights were a major turning point for me. As fantastic as this encounter with Soul Fucker was, it was not real. Once again, I found myself in a situation that yielded only a quick burst of temporary excitement and short-term happiness at best. I had been settling for less than I want in a man and accepting less than I deserve in a relationship ever since my divorce. My addiction to Soul Fucker was another example of settling. I couldn't have him, the way I really wanted him, so I took what I could get. He was like a high-level, superior, VIP Fuck Buddy.

I didn't know much about Soul Fucker's life, other than just the basics. I actually didn't want to know the answers, but of course I wondered, who did he marry? Why? What was she like? What was their relationship like? Why was he here with me? But it was fruitless to think these thoughts. I had entered this situation with eyes (and legs) wide open, and I wasn't going to pretend it was anything more than top-shelf sex. So once I started to enjoy the Soul in Soul Fucker as much as the Fuck in Soul Fucker, I knew I was entering dangerous territory.

I had been in a similar situation before, if you recall. My ex-husband was married when we met. We started our relationship as great friends, obviously with the undercurrent of intense attraction. As our friendship developed, we openly discussed things like love, marriage, our current partners, our dreams and goals. It was a beautiful friendship that turned into a beautiful relationship. It's a damn shame, really, that our marriage didn't work out. I still lament the absence of that magical combination of friendship and loving relationship that we had. I often wonder if there is ever going to be the opportunity for me to share myself with someone as I did with him. Every time I'm in a new relationship and start to think that it just might be possible again, something goes horribly wrong and I lose that hope.

I didn't know enough about Soul Fucker to know if our union had that sort of potential, but a girl knows what a girl feels. Sex is sex. And great sex is great sex. But when there is something else lingering in the corner of the room, call it what you want...connection, feelings, consanguinity, intensity, even a past life-connection...you both know it. Ours was always a lascivious connection at its core. But I had to wonder if we were serving a greater, almost higher purpose for each other. Whatever it was, I can only hope that I served it well for Soul Fucker, and that he will smile that gorgeous, sexy, evil grin when he thinks of our times together.

I hated to let him go, but it wasn't as hard as I thought it would be. It was like giving up sugar. You don't have any emotional attachment to sugar, it's just tops on the list of things you enjoy. You miss it from a physical standpoint, the way it tastes and smells and that moment of erotic pleasure as it melts in your mouth. You savor every bite like it's your last. But, if you never had sugar again, you wouldn't be emotionally devastated; you'd acutely feel its vacancy, while your body would benefit immensely from its absence.

I needed to go out and find some sugar (*read: chocolate*) who was single and available. But how? Oh, right. Tinder!

CHAPTER 32

TINDER, PART *DEUX*

Charlie Brown never met Hector. He seems to think that if he had, he could have identified his issues ahead of time and provided me with a warning. He claims to have an ability to "sniff out the weird." New rule: Charlie Brown has to meet any guy with whom I am about to have a fourth date. A fourth date indicates the beginnings of an actual, regular relationship. If schedule doesn't permit, I am most definitely not permitted to see a guy for a fifth date, nor am I allowed to make any getaway travel plans with anyone before obtaining Charlie Brown's stamp of approval.

This seemed fair. I now had an Ascot Dating Security System like the Slomin Shield: an advanced protocol in place to protect my loved ones and me from unwelcome intruders. I reactivated my Tinder profile knowing that I had air cover.

As you can imagine, since I had been scarred for life by my first Tinder experience, my trepidation level was very high this time around. With each swipe, I held my breath, terrified that I would have to relive that sudden slap in the face when the new face that appeared was the old face of my ex-boyfriend. But swipe, I did. In fact, I swiped my way to something like seventy-five matches over the next few months, with varying levels of post-match action ranging from zero to an actual meeting. Thankfully, not one of those swipes ever again revealed Hector's face or any other part of him.

Tinder is creepy. I feel so strongly about this that my profile says as much. My Tinder profile features the maximum allowable carefully chosen photos (five), my name and age (ahem), and the words "This app is creepy." That simple statement has gotten three distinct reactions from my "matches":

1. A laugh and agreement with a friendly hello.
2. A challenge to explain why I think it's creepy.
3. A defensive comment that it's not creepy at all, it's the greatest thing ever invented, and how dare I?

I have since researched the shit out of reaction number three. Women are exposed to different things than men are on this app and trust me, Tinder *is* creepy. Here is a sampling of things a woman might see on Tinder while innocently swiping in search of a date, a friend, an FTF (friend to fuck), or an LTR (long-term relationship):

- Guy with his left hand outstretched, intentionally displaying his wedding ring, indicating his desire for an affair
- Hairy shirtless guy with a fat gut and no head
- Hairless shirtless guy with great abs and no head
- Underwear photo featuring not-so-impressive

bulge in tighty whiteys or similar unattractive undergarment
- Smiling couple
- Guy you know from work
- Photo of S&M toys in a carefully arranged display
- Giant middle finger (This baffles me. Someone please explain: Is this "fuck you" or "I want to fuck you"?)
- My daughter's summer camp counselor
- Man posing with an infant (wife just had baby and he needs sex with someone)
- Borderline dick picks (This is just a step beyond the underwear/bulge photo.)

In and among these gems were some nice-looking, seemingly stand-up fellows. I felt as if I had gone out for drinks with about seventy-four of my seventy-five matches, sometimes two in one day. I was aggressively dating. There were so many of them, I had to save their names and numbers in my contacts with descriptive codes that referred to their photos and/or profiles, so that I could remember who was who. Unfortunately, there was no need to activate the Ascot Dating Security System for any of them. Here are some highlights—or, rather, lowlights.

- Dan Red Pants seemed great over text. He proclaimed that he was "even better in person" and I figured he might have real potential, so I cleared my night at his suggestion that if drinks went well, we'd end up having dinner. I took a quick shower after work and at the last minute decided to wash my hair so I'd look and feel my best. It takes me a while to blow-dry my hair, so I was running about ten minutes late and I texted him to say so. He texted back, "No problem." I couldn't get a cab so I ended up taking the subway, and again I texted him that I'd get there as soon as I could.

When I arrived nineteen minutes late, panting and apologizing, he was halfway through a drink and not as good looking as his photos. Angrily, Dan Red Pants asked me why I couldn't have managed to be on time. I apologized again and said that I had had to run home to drop off my laptop after work, and then—as I'd explained via text—there were no cabs and I had to take the subway.

"Shit happens, man," was his response. We took seats at the bar and lurched through a very clumsy conversation. Turns out he was the early type, so he had been waiting something like thirty-five minutes, which had set us off on the wrong foot. This guy wasn't the person I'd been texting with. He was shy, quiet, very difficult to talk to. It was like pulling teeth to have a conversation and he kept rubbing his sweaty palms along the thighs of his (not red) jeans. I am usually good in these situations, ever the talk-show host who can get a conversation going with anybody, throw in a few jokes, even involve the bartender for color commentary if necessary. But this guy was not having me at all.

At a certain point, he signaled something to the bartender and I said, "Oh, are you opening a tab?"

"No. I've had enough," said Dan Red Pants, and he grabbed his credit card, quickly scribbled a signature, then got up and left. I scrambled to collect my things and race after him, if only to end things on a more civilized note.

"Pardon me, but did I say something to offend you?" I asked.

"No, I'm just tired. It was nice meeting you."

The whole date lasted thirty-two minutes. For this, I washed my hair?

• I was excited to meet Dwayne Globetrotter, an actual ex-Harlem Globetrotter, but after a few phone conversations that seemed promising, he spelled out his requirements for me becoming his woman as if we were conducting a business deal via text. "Let me be honest. I don't want a relationship, but I want to date someone exclusively. You have to be hot and in shape. You must be available every weekend. I am not available during the week, so don't ask."

• I met police detective Alan for a drink and he was very handsome in his uniform. He had great stories to tell about different roles he'd played as an undercover cop, and his delivery was quirky and entertaining. We made dinner plans about ten different times after the drinks date and even joked about vacationing together. But he never texted or called to follow up on our scheduled meeting days so none of those plans ever materialized. Then one night, while swiping, I came across Detective Alan's photo on Tinder again. This time, he was posing with a smiling petite brunette woman and his profile description read that he and his sexy Latina wife were looking for someone to help spice up their marriage. I guess he had been playing one of his undercover roles with me.

- I met a really nice guy who had nothing wrong with him whatsoever. I went out with him three times because I read somewhere about a dating service in Germany that required you to commit to three dates before you agree to go out with your match. That's how confident they were that you'd eventually hit it off. I figured this guy was worthy of that kind of shot because he truly was a good egg. Each time we met up, I just could not visualize myself having sex with him. Try as I might, I just couldn't do it. Ironically, his name was Tyrone, like my imaginary perfect dude, the recipient of my "Dear Tyrone" letter, who still remained a figment of my imagination.

- One night, I met up with Jay Philly, with whom I had talked and texted for a few weeks. I felt really comfortable with our exchanges and was very much looking forward to meeting him. He was about fifteen minutes late, so I sat at a table at the appointed restaurant and ordered a glass of wine. When he walked in, we greeted each other like we'd been dating for a year: no awkwardness, no fanfare, no "nice to meet you." It was as if we had just seen each other the day before. Jay glanced around the restaurant before he sat down and said, "Did you ask to be seated in the mixed-couple section?" I hadn't noticed, but every table in our immediate vicinity was mixed. "When the waitress asked you if you were waiting on someone, did you say, 'Yes, *my* black man will be here soon.'?" Oh, I loved this guy already.

Jay Philly was a winner. I'd finally met someone who shared my sense of humor, was (around) my age, had an amazing body, a great attitude, was interesting, a single dad, and he regularly left me highly entertaining singing voicemail messages. He lived in my hometown of Philadelphia (duh, from his code name), just blocks from the house where I grew up, and he commuted to New York City for work often.

Problem? Jay Philly just wanted to fuck whenever he was in town, nothing more. And I had enough fuck buddies at my disposal, thanks so much though. Jay and I remained great friends, however, fuck buddy status notwithstanding. The singing voicemails continue, so if you ever call me and my voice mailbox is full, you'll know why.

- I made a dinner date with Ed Car Service and he chose a restaurant off the beaten path on the Lower East Side. It was a rainy night and because he owned a car service, Ed offered to pick me up. But I insisted on meeting him there, and in retrospect, maybe that was a mistake. I was walking down the street with my head down, squinting to read the iPhone Google map to find the joint, while simultaneously trying to hold onto my flapping umbrella in the strong wind. I was rushing so that I would be punctual (having learned my lesson from Dan Red Pants) and not watching where I was walking, and—BAM!—I smacked my crotch into a metal railing at top speed, causing such severe pain I doubled over and almost threw up. When I arrived at the restaurant, panting and sweating, I immediately went to the ladies room to examine my injury and saw a giant, pounding red welt. That pain lasted for no less than three months. I think I had severely bruised the bone. I don't even remember that date. Poor Ed Car Service got eclipsed by my pubic bone accident, excruciating pain, and subsequent bruise. Just thinking about him makes my crotch throb—and NOT in a good way.

- I met Brody Bow Tie for a happy hour drink. This is often my tactic, because it can be a quick one-drink date before I move on to my next activity. If it's good, it leaves us both wanting more. If it's bad, it's an easy exit. This one was the latter. Brody Bow Tie didn't drink, which always creates a bit of a strange dynamic. I really wish these non-drinking Tinder dates would disclose their non-drinking prior to the meet-up. Why invite me out to a "for a drink" and then order a seltzer while I get a buzz alone?

He was from somewhere in the Caribbean (RED ALERT*) and had such a heavy accent that I could barely understand him over the loud music at the lounge he took me to. I have no recollection of what the conversation was about, I just know there was no connection and it was an awkward struggle to hear him. I think this date lasted about fifty-nine minutes before I excused myself to get home to my daughter. He insisted on walking me home but I made him say goodbye about a block away so he wouldn't know where I lived. Then, he would not release me from an uncomfortably long hug. He relentlessly texted and called me for awhile and I politely declined his invitations. When he persisted, I stopped replying and deleted him from my contacts. A few months later, I got a new phone and when I received a text from a number I didn't recognize, instead of ignoring it, I replied, "Who is this, please? I got a new phone." Damn! Here we go again.

For over a year, Brody Bow Tie continued to text me asking when he could see me again. My last reply of "Thanks, but I'm seeing someone now," didn't seem to stick, and then I totally ghosted. You'd think a brotha would get the hint.

- I met Ron The DJ at a bar of my choosing on a busy Friday evening. He thought it was too crowded and suggested we try another spot. I reminded him that I didn't have much time because I'd left my daughter home alone, but he assured me he knew a better place right in the 'hood. I followed him for a few blocks in the pouring rain and wind, which doesn't make for easy walking conversation. His choice was even more packed.

  Ron The DJ and I had a few mutual friends in the music business, so I figured he had potential. He convinced me to jump on the subway "just two stops away" to another place he liked, so I found myself on the jam-packed 6 train, wet and cold from the rain, out of breath trying to keep up with Ron the DJ, who seemed to be on some kind of mission. We arrived at his favorite local bar on the Bowery, only to find it was closed for a private party. By this point, I was ready to just give up. We finally wandered into a wine bar which, thankfully, was perfectly fine until the office party that was occupying most of it started to get rowdy and out of line. I had one glass of wine and excused myself.

  Ron seemed like a really nice guy but after our first-date disaster and a few feeble attempts to set up date number two, he faded away.

• • •

This whole Tinder dating thing was exhausting. I thought I might take a break.

* RED ALERT: It is a known fact among women (or at least between Chloe and me) that men from the Caribbean do not perform oral sex. One night, after Hector and prior to HOGG, I tied one on with a few girlfriends and went dancing at the 40/40 Club where I picked up a Haitian guy with whom I danced all night and danced right into bed. At the moment of truth when I asked him to pleasure me, he said, "Nah, I don't do that." I couldn't get him out of my apartment fast enough. I wish I'd had a snappy comeback, like the one Charlie Brown whipped out when he met Mel Brooks and extended his hand. Mel Brooks said, "I don't shake hands, but we can take a photo together." At which point Ascot zinged back, "I don't take photos."

CHAPTER 33

IT'S NOT JUST ME

It's not just me, you know. Many of my friends, who know that I won't judge them, volunteer stories that are equally if not more horrific than my own frustrating, dating experiences. It's nice to feel like I'm not alone in my weird single-life boat.

RENÉE

My friend Renée met a guy online who seemed great. They got along really well, were the same age, and enjoyed the same simple things: good food, movies, fitness, the usual. Early on, they went to an opening at the Museum of Modern Art, which thrilled her because she is an art buff and it's hard for her to find guys to drag to exhibits she wants to see. Renée (or *Renois*, as I like to call her) was feeling pretty good about this guy's potential.

One night, after a nice dinner about two months into their budding relationship, they went back to her apartment. They were on the couch cuddling and making out and Renée felt happy. She told me at that moment she felt comfortable. There is that moment, thanks to Terry McMillan, when we women know it's OK to exhale. We hold our breath through the first few dates as we observe and learn things about our new man. If things go well, we hold it a bit longer, afraid that something bad might happen. At every step along the way, we remain prepared for the worst. But at a certain point, when things are going well and there have been no ugly surprises, we hit that moment where we release the tension in our shoulders, relax, and let that breath out. Renée was just about to exhale that night on the couch.

Then, he turned to her, looked her in the eye, and said, "I sometimes like to be fucked in the ass by trannies. But I'm not gay."

LAUREN
Lauren's high school sweetheart reached out to her on Facebook. She was thrilled to hear from him after all those years, as she had always loosely categorized him as one that got away. They met for drinks but it turned out he didn't drink. Anymore. He was in recovery. From, like, everything; drinking, drugs, but mostly sex. He was a sex addict, currently in recovery.

ASCOT'S COUSIN
Ascot relayed a few online dating stories from his cousin Earl, a very handsome thirty-eight-year-old gainfully employed and available gentleman who recently moved to New York City from Minneapolis. Why am I not dating Earl?, you ask. This is an excellent question. I must ask Ascot.

Date #1: Earl arrived punctually at the meeting place, where his date was already seated at the bar. She looked exactly like her photos, which is always big relief number one in the online dating world. He sat down next to her and they exchanged pleasantries. He signaled for the bartender's attention, but before the bartender made his way over to take their order, Earl's date gently touched his arm, leaned in closely and whispered into his ear.

"We could have drinks, and order dinner and you might end up spending $150 or so tonight. Instead, you could just give me the $150 and I'll do whatever you want."

Date #2: Once again, Earl met his date at the bar. She, too, was exactly like her photos and things started out well. At mid-drink, she said with a wink, "Do you smoke?"

"Sure," said Earl, "sometimes. Why do you ask?"

"Well," she replied, "I can get you anything you want. To smoke. Or anything else. You know. Just let me know what you want."

First a prostitute, then a drug dealer. What next?

Date #3: Ever the idealist, Earl kept at it. He arrived at the bar for his next date and waited. And waited. He texted his date, "I'm here at the bar. Are you on your way?" She replied instantly, "I'm here. I'm sitting at the end of the bar."

Earl looked down the bar and didn't spot her. He looked up the bar but still didn't see anyone who could possibly be his date. He finally got up, walked to the other side of the bar and saw a woman waving. She looked somewhat familiar but…this woman weighed about 200 pounds. Not what he was expecting, but he gamely trotted over to her.

"Lisa?"

"Yes," she said shyly, and immediately volunteered that the photos online were about ten years old. She explained that she'd gone through a hard time and had gained a lot of weight. "But I'm on a diet," she said cheerfully, "and I have already lost five pounds! I am ready to start dating again."

Always a gentleman, Earl stuck out the evening with Lisa because she was "a nice lady." He bought her a burger and fries, and after she had a couple of light beers in her (maybe this was the diet part), she was pretty funny and quite entertaining. Despite the fact that there was zero romantic connection, Earl still considered his date with "Fat Lisa" time (and money) well spent, unlike the hooker and the dealer. Fat Lisa and Earl remain good friends to this day. Furthermore, Fat Lisa lost about seventy-five pounds and is a real beauty, reclaiming her look from the ten-year-old photos and is now happily dating a fat guy. Earl still calls her Fat Lisa to her face and she roars with laughter every time.

Earl is still online dating. I don't know where he finds his bravery.

CANDACE

My former college roommate, Candy, is divorced and sowing her wild oats like it was 1989 all over again. She is on five different online sites and, much like myself, can't remember who's who. She is and always has been a slut, which is probably why we're friends. She brought home one guy after their second date (this is considered "waiting" in her book), and discovered he was wearing an ankle monitor.

• • •

So, you see, it's not just me. This dating shit is difficult for everyone. After hearing my friends' stories, I started to think that maybe all those guys I met on Tinder and Match and DateABlackGuyWithAJob and Let's Do Lunch were not so bad. I mostly just went out on a bunch of dates with decent guys with whom I had no connection. Good guys, for the most part, but not for me. And that's OK.

Then one morning, while lying in bed next to Soul Fucker (oops, I relapsed), I received this text, verbatim, from an unknown number. (Spoiler: It was Brody Bow Tie. Again.) I have done no editing. With the grammar and punctuation errors that abound, you know it was hard for me to not edit this, but I thought you'd enjoy it more in its raw form:

Good morning gorgeous. Well my dear, I just woke from a dream. A dream where my subconscious became my reality, just for a moment but felt for eternity. In this dream your presence felt... Felt in ways that my heart have so desired from the first time we have encountered. Oh my dear, in this dream of mine we reunited under the heavenly hosts on a lost beach, where the sand are white like snow. There I held your body close to mine, and ogling at you. So beautiful and desirable.

The contour of your exquisite body protrudes so nicely beneath your garments it is almost perfect. Then I gently removed your garments and kiss you from your forehead and slowly to your navel. In your sacred place I laid my wet tongue, to taste of your ambrosia. It tasted so good with the juice dripping out of it.* Then slowly I put my love deep inside you and moved to the motion of our heart beats.

It felt so true and right. With each gentle stoke you held me tighter. With each gentle stroke our bodies temperature rise and ignited that flame between us. Like a covalent bond we became one new element. As I'm pressing deeper and deeper you are biting your lips, and the sound of your mourning sound like music to my ears. Oh my dear just the thought of this while I'm writing this send chills up and down my spine. Such feeling make me want to stroke my manhood. Finally we both got to a place where reached our climax and released ourselves and my strength flew out of me simultaneously holding each other's body closer. After it all done the wave from the ocean came upon on us and washed away our sins...

What a dream... One i long to come true.

This was a text, mind you, not an email. I scrolled for days reading it, especially in my geriatric large text font. Oh Brody Bow Tie, what transpired for you during those fifty-nine minutes that was so vastly different from the fifty-nine minutes I experienced? I showed the text to Soul Fucker who smiled and said, "Guy's got it bad. Do you blame him?"

"Thanks," I replied. "That's not helping."

* *So much for the theory about Caribbean men.*

CHAPTER 34

IMOGEN'S HORNS

My daughter, Imogen, was twelve. She was about to turn thirteen. How the fuck did I have a teenage daughter? The bigger question at the moment, though, was how the fuck did I have a teenage tomboy? How was it possible that a cock-lovin' flagrant heterosexual woman like myself could raise a seemingly stone-cold asexual entity?

Imogen's body, however, suggested otherwise. Her long legs were lean and mean from her martial-arts training. She was uber fit, with upper arms like a gymnast. Her gorgeous, thick, wavy, chocolate-brown hair seemed wasted by being pulled back in a simple low ponytail. Her skin was porcelain, and those naturally perfect eyebrows of hers were obstructed by her thick-framed black eyeglasses.

Yet, this uncompromised beauty chose to wear a black Adidas tracksuit and baggy boy-cut t-shirt every single day of her life. It was a look, for sure, but one that hid her developing teen-girl body. While other girls her age were discovering belly-shirts and short-shorts, my kid could not care less. I was just lucky in this way, I guess.

"You should be thankful," said everyone whose business it was not.

"She'll grow out of it."

"There's no rush, let her be a kid."

"She's so unique, let her do her thing."

Don't get me wrong. I am a flag-waving proponent of "do your own thing," and have always been extremely proud of Imogen for doing hers. And I wasn't in any rush for her to grow up, but I did wonder what was up with all that masculinity.

One day Imogen texted me a photo of Hannah Hart, an Ellen Degeneres-looking Internet personality and comedian. Because she texted me this photo from the opposite end of the living room couch, I was easily able to lift my head up and say, "Why?"

"I like that haircut."

Up until that moment, Imogen had never expressed any desire to do anything with her hair except pull it back into a ponytail. She'd always liked her long hair, never wanted to cut it; but she didn't like it in her face, so it could never be styled either. This was a bit frustrating to me. My gorgeous daughter just didn't seem to care about her looks in the least. I didn't feel the need to rush her into puberty or dress her up like JonBenet, I just thought it might be nice for her to look a little less Pigpen-like during her middle school years. So, her sudden interest in a super-short, angled haircut perplexed me.

Upon further scrutiny of the photo, I saw that one side of Hannah Hart's head was shaved, and this is what appealed to Imogen. I was intrigued by this haircut concept, but how does a mother react to this sudden inquiry without blowing it? I tried to play it cool. I didn't want to get too excited at the possibility of a super-rad haircut for my kid. On the other hand, I didn't like how short it was. Not only was it super butch, but I was pretty sure that, with her wavy hair, Imogen wouldn't be able to replicate that look. So I skated right down the middle, expressing support of the shaved thing but encouraging her to keep her long locks. I Googled no fewer than 943 photos of stylish women with long dark hair, glamorously styled to one side, with the other side shaved. I loved this look and thought it would be amazing on Imogen.

"But I don't like that."

Shot down. There would be no more conversation about her hair. For the moment.

Eventually, the subject weaved its way back into our lives. One of my best friends, Selma (from whom Imogen received her middle name) owns a Madison Avenue hair salon. Selma is like a cool aunt to Imogen, otherwise there would be no circumstance under which Imogen would agree to go to a Madison Avenue hair salon. Selma and about seventeen of her colleagues managed to convince Imogen (as I nodded furiously behind her and made wild hand signals to demonstrate the idea) that she should try a long-hair Mohawk. She would get the shaved look she wanted, keep her long locks, and still be able to wear her hair in a pony tail.

The final result was a tremendous success. It's amazing what a haircut can do. My previously nondescript, all-black-wearing, self-proclaimed nerdish tomboy daughter had transformed her look into one that was hip, stylish, and trendy. Suddenly her track pants and thick-framed glasses made sense. Her ponytail was no longer low and flat, but high up on her head and swinging, revealing two closely shaved sides of her head. A hipster was born.

Imogen had never been a kid who took a long time to get ready. As long as the t-shirt and sweatpants were clean, there was no outfit to put together. It was as if she wore a uniform. After the haircut, I noticed her looking at herself in the mirror more often. Getting her out the door on time for school was a whole new experience.

"What's taking you so long?! Let's go!" I'd yell, and she'd respond that her ponytail had to be exactly in the right spot. Her t-shirts had become a little more fitted and her shapely body was more visible. As she studied herself in the mirror, I wasn't sure if she was appreciating her physique, studying it, liking it, questioning it, or what. Regardless, I was happy to see that she finally cared about her appearance.

Up to that point, Imogen had displayed zero of the typical teenage-girl characteristics: There were no boys, no drama, no silly girlfriends, no fashion issues. She had remained a quiet, studious, childlike bookworm until the moment she decided to shave the sides of her head. Now she was meticulously styling her high ponytail and asking me if she could shave her legs.

• • •

Visualize the following list in a lovely array of alternating bright ROYGBIV rainbow colors, which I unfortunately could not replicate here for printing restriction reasons.

L - Lesbian

G - Gay

B - Bisexual

T - Transgender

T - Two-Spirited

Q - Queer

Q - Questioning

P - Pansexual

P - Polysexual

D - Demisexual

A - Asexual

A - Ally

"What the __k is this?!" I was shocked when I found this colorfully printed list in the home printer tray. And yes, I literally edit myself like how audio drops out on a television or radio broadcast when I curse in front of Imogen. It's a skill I've mastered in order to enjoy the satisfaction of cursing without subjecting Imogen to my foul language. It works; you should try it.

"It's a glossary of terms," Imogen replied flatly.

"Yeah, I can __king see that. Can you please explain why you printed a glossary of terms related to homosexuality?" I kept needing to bleep myself because of the pure surprise.

"It's for my final project in Humanities. Thought I told you."

"No, you didn't tell me. Why are you studying homosexuality in Humanities?"

"We're not studying homosexuality. It's for my final project on LGBT rights."

"Your teacher assigned LGBT rights for your final project?" I knew her school was progressive, but wow.

"No, I chose it."

Now I was really curious. "Why did you choose that subject?" I asked gently.

"I thought it was interesting."

Hmm. At this point, I didn't want to sound unsupportive or accusatory and I certainly didn't want to spook Imogen by asking too many questions that would send her back inside her turtle shell of non-communication.

"Interesting that you find it interesting," that's all I could manage. "What are the other kids doing their projects on?"

"You know...stuff."

My glare clearly indicated that "stuff" was not an acceptable answer.

"Donald Trump. Climate change. Technology."

"Oh, so you were given a list of topics to choose from?" I was starting to see why homosexuality might be the most interesting topic on said list.

"No. Everyone chose their own."

Gulp. "And you chose homosexuality because you thought it was interesting?"

Clearly getting annoyed, Imogen replied, "It's not *homosexuality*. It's *LGBT rights*."

So...was this my cue to question my daughter about

her own sexual orientation? I wasn't prepared to have the conversation at that very moment. She was barely a teenager and hadn't shown any interest in the opposite (nor the same) sex thus far...except when she was in fourth grade and had seemed to have a crush on Tom, who was cute but shy as hell and didn't speak to anyone. "Why do you like that kid when he doesn't even talk?" I'd asked her.

"That's why I like him."

As I've mentioned, she is wise beyond her years.

I decided to leave the LGBT conversation alone for the moment so she could get back to her schoolwork, which Imogen takes very seriously. I cannot claim responsibility for this trait. Of course I encourage her and support her, but her intense academic drive is purely her own. She was obviously putting a lot of effort into the report, judging by the gay rainbow-colored Glossary of Terms. So I let the kid get back to work.

• • •

About a month later, I came home from a meeting in the late afternoon. Imogen was already home after school, doing homework in her room. She seemed like she needed a break, because she immediately came out of her room to greet me. This is a rare event. Usually her teenage self would just remain in her room, headphones on, barely offering a greeting or even acknowledging my presence. Some parents would be annoyed by that lack of interaction, but I am kind of grateful that after we grunt an initial greeting at each other, we go our own ways for a little while, like a grumpy old married couple. When I get home from an intense day, I like to decompress for a minute, even if that means just taking my pants off. That's the first step in getting comfortable—taking my pants off so I can change into my comfy yoga pants. Sometimes I take my pants off in the dining room before I even make it to my bedroom. Imogen finds my undressing routine hilarious. And if my pants are still on by dinnertime, she'll taunt, "Are you going somewhere?"

Anyway, once I'm comfortable, we can interact. But on this particular day, Imogen seemed rather chatty as I walked in, and I didn't want to discourage it. She had an unusually light homework load and was relaxed and not overly grumpy. She followed me into my room and did her usual somersault on my bed.

After I changed into my standard at-home-slob outfit, I plopped down next to her on my bed, playfully falling on top of her. I relished the rare moment of connection. Imogen is a non-hugger, so physical contact is sparse, but sometimes we fist bump or high five; substitutions for hugs or hand-holding that I have come to accept. Occasionally after a high five, our hands linger, which is not actually holding hands—God forbid—but more like an affirmation that we're cool with each other; like she thinks, "You're all right, lady." I never question it, I just roll with it.

We started to chat: How was your day? How was school? Why don't you have a lot of homework? Eventually we got around to the topic of the LGBT rights project on which she was still working.

Gently, I asked, "So how is the project going? Are you glad you chose that topic?"

"It's fine. Interesting."

"You said that before. Why do you find it interesting?"

"I don't know. I just do."

"There is no *reason* you find it interesting?" At this point, we were continuing a high-five, by repeatedly clapping on each other's hands, a steady rhythm that seemed to be driving the conversation. If I stopped clapping her hand, the conversation would stop. I kept clapping gently, rhythmically on her palm.

"No. No reason."

"Are you suuuuuure there is no reason?" I was trying to keep my tone playful and casual.

"Yes, I'm suuuuuure. Why do you ask?"

Clapping continued, "I just want to know *why* you find it so interesting. There are so many interesting topics that you could have chosen. Why this? *Why* do you find it so interesting?" Clap. Clap. Clap.

"Are you asking me if I'm gay?" The clapping stopped.

"Well…" I paused. "Yes. I guess I am." I paused again. "Are you?"

"I don't know. I don't think so." The clapping resumed.

"You don't think so?"

"No. I don't know. I don't know yet. Why?"

"No reason. You don't have to have an answer. You're only thirteen. And you know I don't care, right? You can tell me anything." I wanted her to know that if she was ready to talk about sexuality, or ask questions, that she could. I didn't want to discourage her nor did I want to encourage her. I just wanted her to know that in moments like these, it's OK to tell your mom stuff if you want to. If you don't want to, that's OK, too.

I continued, as did the clapping, "It IS an interesting topic, and I'm proud of you for being so socially conscious and progressive. I was just curious what prompted it, that's all. And I just wonder about your feelings, because you don't seem to have any interest in anyone, boy or girl."

"As far as you know," she replied.

"Oh, snap."

That's all I could muster up at that moment. And then, "Hmph." Do I push? Do I let it go? The clapping had stopped again.

"So…you do like someone?"

"Maybe. Maybe not. Like I said, I don't know yet."

Oh come on! I was just about to roll over on to my pillow, like a teenager myself, and beg her to pleeeeease tell me who she had a crush on—like I was one of her eighth-grade girlfriends. I mean, who's boy-crazier than your own mother? Come on!! Tell meeeeee!!!

Instead I said, "OK, well I guess you'll talk to me if you figure it out. If you want to. Or if you have any questions. OK?"

"OK."

And with that, we bounced out of bed and went to the kitchen to plan dinner. My head was spinning with the non-information that she had just laid on me, but I felt close to her, like we had just had some kind of "talk," even though we hadn't. Or had we?

I knew this must have been a nice moment for Imogen as well, because she rarely comes with me to the kitchen for fear that she might have to help with dinner preparation. But this night, she followed me, talking about school, her classmates, and some kid named Nick who had a man bun. Then she showed me a picture of Nick with the man bun. Then she showed me a picture of Nick without the man bun. Then she showed me another picture of Nick with the man bun. Could Nick be her love interest?

"Oh, he's cute," I said, to see if she would agree.

"No he isn't," she snapped back, "eww. "Why do you think he's cute? Eww."

Actually I didn't think he was all that cute. I thought of showing her a picture of Soul Fucker on the local gym website and saying, "You want to see cute? *This* is cute." But of course those are lines that shall not be crossed. My brain only thinks of these things to amuse itself. And to distract itself from heavy and serious moments like the one that sort of, almost just happened.

CHAPTER 35
MAD ABOUT MEN

They say (those same motherfuckers again?) that confession is good for the soul. I believe this to be true. It's what Chloe suggested I do: Concentrate on me-time, write my stories, get it all out, and do a little self-examination in the process. It feels good to look inside and just accept what's there, dirty deeds and all, and to spill out all the adventures in a hopefully humorous catharsis without offending *everyone*.

But it's scary to allow others to read your personal confessions. People judge, they can't help it. So by spilling all these stories out, I am exposing parts of myself that are maybe not so lovely. I risk changing the way people view me. What can I say? I'm honest. You might not like my truth, and you might be a little judgmental because you can't help it (that's OK, I get it), but at least you know it's the truth. Telling the ugly truth is one thing when it's in your own "Untitled" folder on your desktop that no one reads (except your nosy, snooping ex-boyfriend), but once you decide to share it, whether with your friend Chloe or with the whole world, you're entering scary territory. You have two giant balls, for sure.

Speaking of giant balls, I have some nerve. In another

attempt at a creative endeavor, I host a weekly radio show segment called *Mad About Men*, in which I comment on relationship issues and disseminate advice to listeners on various love-related topics and dating. Me. The one whose relationship road has been so very bumpy. Actually, it's not even a road. It's more like one of those wild theme-park roller coaster rides that take you soaring higher than you can imagine, then plunge downward until your heart is in your throat, then twist and turn until you are nauseous. It's fun and exciting in the beginning, then you question why the fuck you're even on this thing, and finally you just want it to end already. Once the ride is over, you look back over your shoulder at it and wonder if you want to get on it again, despite that you are still nauseous. Me. And yet I host a radio show in which I offer advice on relationships. Behold the irony.

Still, maybe my hardened and jaded, no-nonsense, non-romantic and practical approach to relationships can provide new, clear perspective for the next dumb bitch in line for the roller coaster. *Mad About Men* also tackles subjects to help men when dealing with said dumb bitch.

There was that time when one of my girlfriends at work was lamenting over a guy she'd dated for a few months who had stopped calling her. We were in the office lunchroom when I flat out said, "It's over, Amy. Just realize that. Stop analyzing every little thing he does. If he wanted to be with you, he would be. It's as simple as that. Move on, dammit." And I made her cry, right there amongst our lunching co-workers.

Years later, Amy thanked me. Deep down, she had known I was right. She needed to hear those harsh words pushing her to move on, which she eventually did. Now, she is happily married to a totally different guy she met shortly thereafter. They have two beautiful kids and I rest my case.

Anyway, in *Mad About Men*, the radio show, I try to bring my experience to listeners in the same way that I did with Amy—with straight-up, honest, call-it-like-it-is commentary. Sometimes I address listeners' emails, other times I bring in a topic to discuss and debate with callers. The show always generates lively conversation from which my co-host, the listener, or I myself learn something new— or at the very least, we all have a good laugh.

• • •

I recently attended a brunch in honor of my cousin. She was pregnant with her second kid and, instead of a traditional baby shower, she'd requested a simple brunch with only A-listers attending. There were nine of us, a diverse group of women ranging in age from thirty-one to sixty-one, and everyone was married. Except me.

After a few mimosas, the conversation really started flowing. My cousin mentioned my radio show and how much she loves the topics I discuss. She told everyone they should tune in, at which point, one of her friends piped up and said, "HEY! *I* have a topic for your show! MY HUSBAND IS AN ASSHOLE." Everyone laughed. Then she said, "No, really. My husband is an asshole."

I was shocked when *all but one* of the others at the table chimed in to say that their husbands were, on some level, *also assholes*. The only one who stayed quiet was the pregnant guest of honor.

These ladies weren't asking me for advice, nor what to do about their asshole husbands; they were just resigned to the fact that their husbands were assholes of varying degrees. I suspected this was a rare environment for each of them, one in which they felt completely comfortable to speak their minds about their asshole husbands. No one was judging, no one disagreed, no one offered unsolicited advice, no one was shocked. In fact, we all barely even reacted. We were a group of different women—of all sizes, shapes, ages, and backgrounds—relating to each other. It was truly a special moment. When people meet one another for the first time, find common ground, and connect—that's one of my favorite things in the world. Second only to the afterglow of mind-blowing sex.

One woman was separated and moving out the very next day. One was in the middle of divorce proceedings. One had been separated from her husband for the last year, but they had recently gotten back together after he did some soul searching and spent some time at an Ashram retreat, where he discovered his "ohm place," as she called it. We asked her if things were better now, assuming he was a new man, and she said, "Nope. He's still just as much of an asshole."

The sixty-one-year-old at the table stayed quiet for a long time, smiling knowingly as she listened to the others. When our attention eventually turned to her, she said that her husband of forty years had always been an asshole, from day one.

"So why did you marry him, then?" we all wanted to know.

"He said he was going to be rich!" she said.

The table erupted in laughter. But she wasn't joking.

"Forty years later, he is still an asshole, and he's still not rich."

Silence for a second, then one of the ladies asked her why she didn't leave him. (Oh wait, that was no lady, that was me.) Her response was that after investing forty years of her life in this asshole, raising his kids and taking care of his home, she didn't feel she had that option. She needed the stability and solid ground that the marriage provided.

The mid-divorce woman had had enough of this bullshit and was frantically pulling up Match.com on her phone, insisting that we create a profile for the lovely, long-married lady so that she could find herself a boyfriend. At least she might enjoy a modicum of happiness, while she stuck it out with her asshole.

You might think she said, "Oh, noooooo. I couldn't do such a thing." Instead, she smiled coyly, shrugged her shoulders, and leaned over to take a look at that Match. com app.

So you see, this kind of shit doesn't really do much to motivate me toward chasing that traditional long-term relationship goal. I was married once, you saw where that got me. And where did it get these bitches? Despite all the moaning about being single that I've done in these 200-ish pages, I might just be better off in my current state. Freedom, independence, self-sufficiency, and autonomy sound a hell of a lot more appealing than being married to an asshole for forty years.

So, if I never stumble across this extraordinary unicorn (possibly called Tyrone or similar) who can appreciate that I am who I am—either because of everything that I've been through, or I've been through everything because of who I am—that's just fine. I'll continue to email Chloe all my deep thoughts for a laugh or a cry. I'll hit up the gym or Tinder every once in a while to see who's DTF (Down to Fuck, a horribly crass expression I'd prefer not to use, but it serves the purpose). I'll have brunch with my girlfriends for good cock talk *Sex and the City*-style (but with less bitchiness and more diversity). I'll offer advice via email to all my younger single friends who have no game. I'll continue to address *Mad About Men* listeners in hopes that I might have some kind of positive impact. I'll hope that my kid still wants to hang out with me when she's older so we can be like those moms and daughters who call each other "best friends." But most important, I hope that I can impart some of the knowledge I have gained on my journey to my precious Imogen, when she's ready to receive it, so that she doesn't have to endure anywhere near the heartbreak and misadventure that I have. Sometimes I fear it's too late for me, but it's just the beginning for her. And, despite all that I have been through and all the relationship and life lessons I have learned, I fear that I am still ill-equipped to help her. Imogen's individual journey will be all her own, but maybe, just maybe, I can offer a sliver of wisdom to make it more bearable for her.

CHAPTER 36

DEAR HAPPY SELF

Email to...No One.

Dear Happy Self,

If you exist, then congratulations. This is the moment you have been striving for and I want to commend you on your success. Now let's get real.

Do not ever take your happiness for granted. You must appreciate every day, every moment. Don't get complacent and forget all the work and energy that got you to this moment. Appreciate it, revel in it, thank the universe every day for it.

As we well know, it wasn't easy to get here. After all the trials and tribulations, sadness, defeat, hoping, praying, holding your breath... you made it. Periodically remind yourself of what it took to get here. Don't forget how elusive happiness can be, how hard you must work for it, and how patient you have to be to sustain it. As The Weeknd said, "You Earned It." (Is this song reference dated or even comprehensible now? Trust me, it was hot shit when I wrote this.)

Happiness can all go away in a flash. After years of work and toil, in a blink of an eye, it can be destroyed. This is also why you must appreciate every moment, and never take happiness for granted.

I write this letter to you, Happy Self, from a different place. I have not yet arrived to where I know you live. I envy you, with your happiness, Happy Self. I cannot wait to become you. For now, I am patient, hopeful, confident. I no longer live in the sad places, and I am well on my way to that happy destination.

Where you live, Happy Self, I will be self-fulfilled, without relying on any man to fill a hole (other than the obvious one). I've been self-sufficient for my whole life, but being self-fulfilled is different. It would be nice to have some company, but being self-fulfilled means that I don't need it. If that company comes in the form of friends, family, or just myself (I have been my own best friend for a long time), that works, too.

So, Happy Self, if you're reading this and you're a happy version of me, then congratulations. You did it. Don't ever forget what it took to get here and keep on striving for bigger and better cock...oops, I mean...things. It sounds like you are on the right path. I always knew you could do it.

I hope to meet up with you soon.

Love,

Me

GLOSSARY

HDT: *Hot Dominican Trainer; "bang" in the beginning*

MD: *Major Dick; aka, Ethan, dated for five years*

HMN: *Hot Male Nurse; dated on and off during above five years*

HCT: *Hot Cuban Trainer; nada aqui*

C-LO: *Nickname for best friend Chloe; invented prior to "J-Lo" or "CeeLo" were known*

ASCOT: *Nickname for other best friend Charlie Brown (as if he needs one with a name like that)*

DEL TACO: *Verb; to confront your significant other with accusations of shady behavior; to be in a generally uncomfortable situation in your relationship*

SOUL FUCKER: *Your deepest undoing*

FUCK BUDDY: *A substance-free sexual partner; refer to chapter of same name for identifying characteristics*

HFA: *Hot Flight Attendant*

CFA: *Cute Flight Attendant (same as above)*

Mr. HH: *Actual initials of actual boyfriend*

FREDDY: *Everyone's name with whom you get set up on a date through "Let's Do Lunch" Dating service, which is never lunch*

HOGG: *Hot Office Ghana Guy*

BBC: *Big black cock*

DTF: *Down To Fuck, but actually, no one is really using this expression anymore*

HAPPY SELF: *Definition unknown at this writing*

ACKNOWLEDGEMENTS & THANKS

Chloe - This is all your fault. I only wanted to make you laugh in some damn emails, but you enjoyed them too much. Thank you from the bottom of my heart for being on the receiving end of my stories. Thank you for your patience, understanding, true friendship, and for making Ant's room my room, always. You are my #1 main bitch.

Danielle and Bryan - Thanks for letting me use your dining room table to write a lot of this; and to Chloe and Luke, who coincidentally have the same dining room table.

Marty Maidenberg - Thanks for your words, advice, wisdom, love, support and everything else under the sun that you've provided to me over the (many) years. You're a true friend. Also, I stole your Mel Brooks joke, thanks, I'll buy dinner.

Christopher Robbins - You are "defiantly" funnier than I could ever make you out to be, sorry about that. Thank you for being a great sounding board, for everything, always. Can you please call fake Earl, already?

BBS - Thank you for your encouragement and support while I wrote a damn book...without your even reading a word of it. Maybe you could read it now, though? You were a big part of the whole process, and aren't you glad you're not in it? Well, maybe you are. I guess you'll have to read it to find out.

Morgan White-Bread - Thanks for believing so hard. If nothing of our project ever materializes, know that I consider your belief in me, your encouragement, and support a big win.

Jason Morgan - I should give you some kind of credit, no? I stole your jokes and made them my own. Also, your name. Thanks for both. And, you *could* have been Tyrone, but nah. I love you like a play cousin.

Janice Deaner, Natalie Jason - Also your faults, who knew? Sincere thanks.

Mike Flannery - I hope I didn't offend you and your feelings.

Thanks to my *husband*—who is actually my ex-husband and currently someone else's husband, but until I get a new husband, he will still be considered my husband because he's the only husband I ever had—for leaving me, because otherwise I would not have written this book. Also, no thanks to him, as well.

To all the *men* who are portrayed here: Sorry, not sorry.

To any *family members* who might read this: it's all fiction, honest.

Very special thanks to **_Laura Ross_** for your tough love. You forced that Oxford comma on me, and now I'm ruined for life (see?). And, yes, I may be old school with my two spaces in between sentences like when I typed on an IBM Selectric, but you still have an AOL address, so whatever. Thank you for making me look inward, and then go deeper than any of the men ever went.

BOOK-CLUB DISCUSSION QUESTIONS

Warning: Do not operate questions without cocktails (yes, I said COCKtails) and/or wine. Alcohol may improve results.

1. Is Madelyn a slut? Do you have empathy for her? Can you relate to her?

2. How does Madelyn differ from you? How is she the same? Would you be friends with her?

3. Do you believe all this shit is actually true?

4. What disparaging acronymic nickname would you give your ex- or current romantic partner?

5. How do you feel about Amtrak, red wine, and anal sex (not necessarily at the same time)?

6. Do you like big black cocks? Discuss and compare stories.

7. What was your favorite passage or episode and why? Suggestions: Therapy Cock, Getting into My Drawers.

Or, did you prefer the more serious stuff, such as Glass Balls or Once More With (Less) Feeling?

8. Do you have or have you ever had a fuck buddy? Tell everyone all the details. All of them.

9. How do you feel about the ending? Do you think Madelyn will ever find her man, or is it hopeless for this bitch?

10. What advice would you give to Madelyn? (In fact, can you please email her directly with some advice or if you want to set her up with anyone? madaboutmen98@gmail.com).

BONUS QUESTIONS:

a. For white girls: Have you ever slept with a black guy? If not, would you? Why or why not?

b. For black girls: Have you ever slept with a white guy? If so, why on earth would you do that?

ABOUT THE AUTHOR

Madelyn Morgan is a music business marketing executive. After years of using her creative talent for the benefit of  others, she decided to focus on her first love, writing. She also hosts a weekly radio segment (her second love), also called *Mad About Men*, which airs on WIYY, Baltimore. Morgan lives in New York City with her teenage kid (her *true* love), who is not allowed to read this book until she's 18. Maybe 21. Maybe never.

CPSIA information can be obtained
at www.ICGtesting.com
Printed in the USA
LVOW10s0205270617
539399LV00002B/315/P

9 780998 297705